KU-779-771

Book No......................... Class No./Mark ....
791.43025
This book is to be returned on or before the last date
stamped below.

16. ... 2001

15 JAN 2002

-8 MAY 2002

2 4 MAR 2003

2 8 APR 2003

-9 NOV 2004
16. APR 07

WITHDRAWN
FROM STOCK

production design
& art direction

screencraft

430727

peter ettedgui

production design
& art direction
screencraft

RotoVision

A RotoVision Book

Published and distributed by RotoVision SA

Rue du Bugnon 7

CH-1299 Crans-Près-Céligny

Switzerland

RotoVision SA, Sales & Production Office

Sheridan House, 112/116A Western Road

Hove, East Sussex BN3 1DD, UK

Tel: +44 (0)1273 727 268

Fax: +44 (0)1273 727 269

E-mail: sales@rotovision.com

Copyright © RotoVision SA 1999

All rights reserved. No part of this publication may be reproduced, stored in a
retrieval system or transmitted in any form or by any means, electronic, mechanical,
photocopying, recording or otherwise, without permission of the copyright holder.

ISBN 2-88046-364-5

10 9 8 7 6 5 4 3 2 1   27.95

Series devised by Barbara Mercer

Design Copyright © 1998 Morla Design, Inc., San Francisco

Layout by Artmedia, London

Production and separation by ProVision Pte. Ltd., Singapore

Tel: +65 334 7720

Fax: +65 334 7721

contents

introduction

"It's one of those foolish truisms that a lot of what is perceived as great cinematography actually is really good production design or really good location choice. Often it's that easy – it's so damn good, just photograph it." Director of photography Stuart Dryburgh's comment in **Cinematography** is an appropriate curtain-raiser to this second title in the SCREENCRAFT series. It's true that the cinematography of a film often attracts more attention than its design, with the D.P. receiving more of the glory (and the money) than the production designer. This is partly due to the fact that the basic tools of cinematography – the camera, light and shadow – are the key raw materials of cinema. The role played by design is less tangible, as Richard Sylbert, perhaps the most influential of contemporary American designers, acknowledges: "If someone says 'cinematographer', you think, oh yeah, that's the guy who does the camerawork. 'Costume designer' – that's also easy to define. But what is a 'production designer'? It's a title searching for a definition."

Léon Barsacq, the great French art director and historian of film design, identified 1908 as a key year in the evolution of film design. Until then, Barsacq observed, the camera had been an immobile spectator of a film's action, which would unfold as if behind the proscenium arch of a theatre. Early film design simply borrowed theatre techniques such as painted scenery. But in 1908, the camera was removed from the fixed moorings of the tripod and began actually to enter the action and move around within it (as if it were one of the characters). It was the end of filmed theatre and the beginning of cinema, and it obliged the film-makers to construct more realistic and three-dimensional sets in order to preserve the illusion. The emergence of design as a specific film-making craft was further benefited by the fact that at around the same time, the miracle of "moving pictures" was becoming less of a novelty in itself to audiences. Directors and producers now had to seek new ways to satisfy the audience's hunger to be shown something they'd never seen before. Throughout the 'teens and 1920s, the designer (whose official title was "art director") played a pivotal role as cinema became increasingly ambitious in scale and spectacle, reaching early peaks with **Cabiria** in Italy (1913, art directed by Camillo Innocenti), **Intolerance** in the U.S. (1916, art directed by Frank Wortman and Ellis Wales), **The Ten Commandments** (1923, art directed by Paul Iribe), **Metropolis** in Germany (1925, art directed by Otto Hunt, Erich Keitelhut and Karl Vollbrecht) and **Napoléon** in France (1927, art directed by Alexandre Benois and Pierre Schild). Thanks largely to the work of such craftsmen and their art departments, cinema could now bring the past vividly to life. It could transport one to exotic locales (such as Monte Carlo, recreated in 1921 by Richard Day on the back-lot of Universal Studios for **Foolish Wives**). It could reveal astonishing visions of the future.

During the golden age of the studio system in America and Europe, films were made entirely on the studio lot. Interiors were built on the stages; exteriors were shot on the back-lot. "We used to build everything – city exteriors for London, Paris, New York, wherever," Henry Bumstead recalls of the art department at Paramount. "One day you might do something in the Gothic style, next day, art nouveau." Hollywood art directors like Bumstead worked under the head of the art department who supervised the art direction of every production made at the studio, and who was responsible for creating a house-style for the studio (each Hollywood major had its own look). The art department's stylistic influence was further boosted by the advent of colour, which created new expressive possibilities in film design. In 1939,

this burgeoning influence was given full recognition for the first time by David O. Selznick, producer of **Gone with the Wind**. Richard Sylbert recounts how the film's pioneering art director, William Cameron Menzies, controlled the look of every scene in the film through detailed storyboards which were rigorously adhered to. In acknowledgement of Menzies' vital contribution to his great Hollywood epic, Selznick credited him as the film's "Production Designer".

As more art directors subsequently became known as production designers, their assistants inherited the cast-off title of art director. While the former was responsible for the overall design of a film, the latter managed the art department's budget and schedule and supervised the construction of the sets, from the drafting office to the studio stage. This division of labour has largely persisted to the present day, although the distinction is sometimes blurred. John Beard and Nigel Phelps, two designers featured in this book, were employed as art directors early in their careers, but in fact worked more as secondary designers. To compound the confusion, the American Academy of Motion Picture Arts and Sciences still gives its Oscar "for best art direction".

Ironically, it was not long after the advent of the new and grand title of production designer that broader developments and forces in world cinema apparently began to diminish the contribution of the art department. At the close of the Second World War, the Italian neo-realist film-makers heralded a new era by shooting their films entirely in real locations (while the Cinecittà Studios in post-war Rome served as a camp for displaced persons). Their example inspired the *nouvelle vague* directors in France who also abandoned the studio stages in favour of the streets. Their call to arms – nothing short of a rebellion against the rigid, studio-based practices of their predecessors – was in turn taken up by the independent cinema movements which flourished everywhere in their wake. In America, the golden age of the Hollywood studios was drawing to a close by the late-1950s and the influence of the new spirit in cinema was manifested in such counter-culture films as **Bonnie and Clyde** (1967) and **Easy Rider** (1969). Apart from the added vitality and realism gained by shooting outside the confines of the studio lot, it was also a lot cheaper to do so. The inevitable knock-on effect, however, was the demise of ground-up production design in which entire worlds were created from scratch by the art department in the studio.

French designer Dan Weil reflects on the problem of beginning a career as a production designer in the film-making culture bequeathed by the new wave: "People in the French film industry thought of cinematography as a technical craft which required years of study; but after the *nouvelle vague*, they believed that anyone could design a set – a friend of the director, his cousin, or girlfriend – whoever. After all, everyone buys things for their apartment, or has some basic knowledge of how to do a place up." Designing period movies, meanwhile, was seen largely as a question of hiring the appropriate stately home. Richard Sylbert is not impressed by this kind of "production design": "I know people who get Oscars for renting country houses," he

comments wryly. "The National Trust should have more Oscars than most designers in England."

The production designers who appear in the following pages, however, are men and women who have helped to reinvent the role of design in contemporary cinema. "I am not interested in decor *per se*," American designer Patrizia von Brandenstein states in her chapter, "the most beautiful ballroom on earth means nothing unless it helps the context of the story." Like many of her fellow contributors to this title, von Brandenstein's design process is concerned with distilling a visual concept from the screenplay's thematic, emotional and psychological concerns. This concept becomes the determining factor in all the designer's aesthetic choices: the mass and volume of a set, the source of the light, the choice of locations, the colours, fabrics, textures and props in the dressing. In order to create a cohesive look for a film, all these elements must resonate with one another and evoke an atmosphere appropriate to the story and the characters. "It's important to understand," says British designer Stuart Craig, "that the designer of a film has nothing to do with interior design or fashion. We are serving a dramatic art."

Craig also identifies another vital function of his job: "If the title 'production designer' requires justification, then I've always thought that we deserve it because we have to design not only the images, but the way the money and the effort is expended. The designer is absolutely pivotal in helping the producer and director find a way to make the film." This rarely-acknowledged aspect of film design involves reconciling the requirements of the screenplay with the film's budget and schedule. It requires the designer to make critical decisions about what can be found and shot on location, and what needs to be shot in the studio. Sometimes it is impossible to shoot in the actual location specified by the story (Dante Ferretti recounts in his chapter how the Indian and Chinese authorities conspired to prevent **Kundun** being made in India); in this scenario, the designer must recreate the location in another country (Morocco eventually stood in for Tibet in **Kundun**). The designer must also decide how much of a set needs to be built; and how much can be created through other techniques such as forced-perspective scene painting, matte painting or the new tool of CGI (computer-generated imagery). "The major decisions one makes as a designer affect not just the look of the film, but the entire production process," Craig concludes.

In both aesthetic and practical terms, then, we can define the role of the production designer as being the architect of the illusions depicted on the screen. Sometimes, the nature of the illusion demands that the design is as much a star of the film as its principal cast; who can forget Ken Adam's War-Room in **Dr Strangelove** or his Fort Knox gold vault in **Goldfinger**? Likewise, the spectacular, haunting vision of Gotham City by Anton Furst (and his art director Nigel Phelps) in **Batman**, or Richard Sylbert's richly atmospheric evocation of 1930s' Los Angeles in **Chinatown**? Science fiction, fantasy, musicals, and period films offer the most obvious platform for eye-catching design, but it should be remembered that even if the subject is contemporary, or the style emulates documentary,

we are still witnessing an illusion which has been designed. "Film stories, even when they are taken from life, are fictions," Allan Starski avers in his chapter. "The designer's responsibility is to make the audience believe that the artifice they are watching is real." Some of the most successful film design is the least obvious – the character-driven design of Wynn Thomas in **Do the Right Thing**, or Dean Tavoularis' spare but meticulous work on **The Conversation**.

For too long, the vital contribution of the production designer has not been properly acknowledged by scholars and critics who write about the film medium; or has been confused with the work of the director or the cinematographer. The aim of this book is both to clarify the role of design in film, and to celebrate some of the great practitioners of the craft. The contributors to **Production Design & Art Direction** span three generations of film-making. Through Henry Bumstead's recollections, we are transported back into the art department during the heyday of the Hollywood studio system, while Ken Adam and Richard Sylbert, both protégés of William Cameron Menzies, connect us with the founding father of production design as well as pointing to its future. As with this title's predecessor **Cinematography**, we have endeavoured to include film artists whose collaborations with directors have enriched not only their own craft, but also have influenced profoundly the look of modern cinema: Ken Adam with Stanley Kubrick, Dean Tavoularis with Francis Ford Coppola, Dante Ferretti with Federico Fellini, Ben van Os with Peter Greenaway, John Beard with Terry Gilliam, Cao Jiuping with Zhang Yimou and Christopher Hobbs with Derek

Jarman are some of the examples in the following chapters. Meanwhile, the films discussed by our contributors encompass period, contemporary and futuristic subjects. They range from mainstream studio projects to independent films made with shoestring budgets, and represent both narrative drama and more experimental, conceptual work. Film is an international medium, and the last factor which influenced our selection was that the contributors should represent several film-making cultures; the book features designers from the U.S., France, Britain, Sweden, Holland, Italy, Poland and China.

Apart from thanking the 16 designers for sharing their insights and experience with us and also for contributing the wealth of sketches, paintings, photographs, storyboards and technical drawings that appear in the following pages to illustrate their aesthetic principles and working methods, we would also like to thank their agents, assistants, partners and friends who have made it possible to liaise with them despite their busy schedules. Our gratitude in this respect is particularly due to Monica Phelps and Xiao Han. John Snow, a scenic artist who works with Patrizia von Brandenstein, supplied many of the production shots featured in her chapter; Stephenie McMillan, Stuart Craig's set decorator, likewise provided photographs documenting their work. Dave Kent at the Kobal Collection and Martin Humphries at Ronald Grant Archive researched many of the stills required to supplement the material loaned to us by the contributors. APM Photography photographed many of the designers' material. Eloyse Tan, Man Sai Karina Hui and Wai Chi Lee

provided the translations into and from Chinese which enabled a two-way communication with Cao Jiuping. Judith Burns at The Home Office supplied the transcriptions of the interviews which provided the basis for each chapter's text. Andrea Bettella at Artmedia developed the book's layouts (based on the styling created by Morla Design for the series), giving shape and cohesion to the diversity of visual and textual elements.

Lastly, I would like to express my gratitude to the editorial team at RotoVision – Natalia Price-Cabrera, Kate Noël-Paton, Zara Emerson, Alannah Moore and Barbara Mercer – who together have shared the mammoth task of working with the contributors in order to research, assemble, catalogue and edit the rarely-seen visual material featured in this volume. Like a feature film, the SCREENCRAFT books are the product of a collaborative effort, and without the commitment, expertise and enthusiasm of this team, the series would not be possible.

PETER ETTEDGUI

biography

Henry Bumstead, who began his career in the Hollywood studio system, remains as active as ever today, his craftsmanship and artistry sought out by directors such as Clint Eastwood – for whom he has designed **Joe Kidd** (1972), **High Plains Drifter** (1973), **Unforgiven** (1991), **Midnight in the Garden of Good and Evil** (1997), **True Crimes** (1999) and **Space Cowboys** (2000) – and Martin Scorsese

henry bumstead

(**Cape Fear**, 1991). Working at Paramount (1937–1960) and Universal (1961–1983), he designed films in every genre – war movies, thrillers, westerns, musicals, comedies, gangster films. He collaborated with Anthony Mann (**The Furies**, 1950), Nicholas Ray (**Run For Cover**, 1954), Frank Tashlin (**Hollywood or Bust**, 1956), Michael Curtiz (**The Vagabond King**, 1956 and **The Hangman**, 1959), Abraham Polonsky (**Tell Them Willie Boy is Here**, 1969) and Billy Wilder (**The Front Page**, 1974). His collaboration with Robert Mulligan yielded, *inter alia*, **To Kill a Mockingbird** (1962), winning him his first Oscar. His second was earned for **The Sting** (1973), one of several films he designed for George Roy Hill. Perhaps his most important collaboration was with Alfred Hitchcock – they worked on **The Man Who Knew Too Much** (1954), **Vertigo** (1958), **Topaz** (1969) and **Family Plot** (1976), as well as several unrealised projects. Bumstead's "knack for colour" is seen to brilliant effect in the earthy palette of **The Sting** and reds and greens of **Vertigo**.

interview

I started out in the business at the height of The Depression. I studied architecture and fine arts at the University of Southern California, and at the end of my sophomore year, I got a job in the art department of RKO. Now, I was born in Ontario, California, population 10,000 people – I was a real country bumpkin. In those days, movies were about wonderful stories, beautiful sets, beautiful people. You could leave your ordinary, drab life and go see magic. So when I got on that RKO lot and saw people like Gary Cooper walking around, the bug bit me. After I graduated from USC, I was interviewed and hired by Hans Dreier, head of the art department at Paramount Studios – the luckiest moment of my life. Dreier came over to Hollywood in the early '30s from UFA studios in Berlin with other émigrés (including the likes of Fritz Lang, Ernst Lubitsch, von Sternberg and Marlene Dietrich).

Paramount was like a small city with department after department to aid you in your job. The studio system was

(1–12) **Vertigo**: (1) Art department illustration of Bumstead's design for James Stewart's apartment, built in the studio with translite backing for the window view of San Francisco's Coit Tower. (3) Hitchcock's original sketch of the view. When Bumstead asked, "Why Coit Tower?" Hitchcock replied, "Because it is a phallic symbol." (2) Bumstead's design for the villain's San Francisco club and (4) Hitchcock's original sketch.

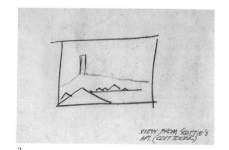

VIEW FROM SCOTTIE'S
APT. (COIT TOWER)

11

(11) Exterior of Mission San Juan Bautista, scene of two major sequences. The tower didn't exist at the location; it was created as a matte painting. (5–10) Mission tower storyboard: Stewart pursues apparently suicidal heroine Kim Novak. Stricken by vertigo, he is unable to prevent her plunging to her death. In reality, the suicide is an elaborate deception: it is the villain's wife (who Novak was impersonating) who has been thrown from the top of the tower. The storyboard enabled the production to break down a complex dramatic scene requiring location shots, studio shots and footage of a scale model (needed to execute the pioneering simultaneous track in/zoom out camera move used to simulate vertigo). (12) Plan for overhead shot from top of tower which ends the storyboarded scene.

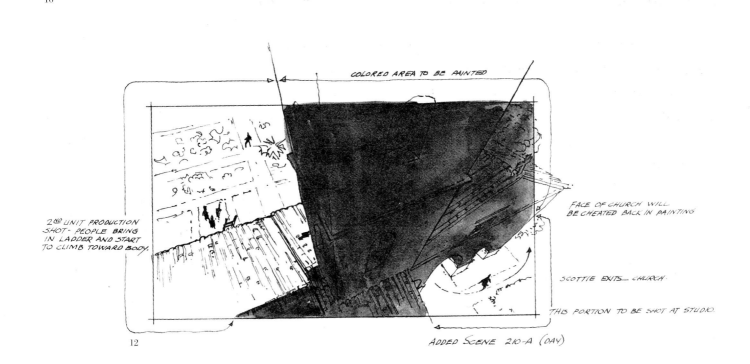

COLORED AREA TO BE PAINTED

2ND UNIT PRODUCTION SHOT- PEOPLE BRING IN LADDER AND START TO CLIMB TOWARD BODY.

FACE OF CHURCH WILL BE CHEATED BACK IN PAINTING

SCOTTIE EXITS CHURCH.

THIS PORTION TO BE SHOT AT STUDIO.

12

ADDED SCENE 210-A (DAY)

1

(1–3) **The Sting**: Bumstead drew on his own memories of
The Depression ("everything seemed brown in those days"),
as well as Walker Evans' photographs of the period. The
palette of rusty reds and leathery browns gave the film its
evocative patina. Bumstead collaborates closely with the D.P.,
set decorator and costume designer in order to develop an
integrated colour palette for each film he works on.

2

3

wonderful – you felt like you were part of a big family, and the studio really cared for its employees. I knew almost everyone on the lot – not only carpenters and painters, but cameramen, writers and actors. There was an apprentice system in almost every department so you could really learn your trade. In the art department, you got to do everything – sketching, drafting, building models. While working on **Dr Cyclops**, I learned about creating effects shots from Ernest Schoedsack, co-director of **King Kong**, as well as from Hitchcock, who loved forced-perspective tricks like having a midget in a small car running through the background (to maintain the correct scale with the forced-perspective). When I designed the houseboat climax of **Cape Fear** for Martin Scorsese (we built a tank for the sequence in Fort Lauderdale), he'd never done a matte shot before. He'd never used a gimbal. He was like a kid with a new toy. But in the old days, such devices were part of our everyday work. We used to build everything on the lot – city exteriors for London, Paris, New York, wherever. We learned how to reproduce details in all architectural styles; one day you might have to do something Gothic, next day, art nouveau. You had no choice about what you worked on; I could have been assigned to **Sunset Boulevard** if it hadn't overlapped with another picture I was doing. But then in my wildest dreams, I wouldn't have imagined working with Alfred Hitchcock. As far as I'm concerned, he is one of the truly great directors.

Hans Dreier instilled a strong work ethic in his art directors. We were taught to be the first on the stage every morning. Everyone wore suits in those days (once, I turned up to a meeting with Hitchcock wearing a spotted sports shirt; without so much as a good morning, Hitch said: "You! You look like you have cirrhosis of the liver!" I went home and changed). We'd spend a couple of hours preparing a set for the day's shooting. Then we'd be back in the office, designing or drafting, trying to get the budget down – the legendary producer Hal Wallis taught me the importance of being financially responsible; he never wasted money on his pictures, even big ones like **Casablanca** – or at the mill supervising construction, always working ahead of the rest of the company. In the evening, we'd check in on the shoot. So the day would be spent running from stage to stage on the lot; a good way to stay skinny. Apart from teaching me the value of hard work, Hans Dreier also taught me the two most valuable lessons I ever learned. My first picture as art director was **Saigon**. The opening set was a waterfront bar. I went down to the Paramount research department where there were photographs of everything – except bar interiors in Saigon. So I used my imagination. I designed the bar with shutters and fans and batwing doors like a saloon. "Outside", I had a cut-out of a ship's stern (we used cellophane to create the effect of the sea) against a scenic backing of what I thought Saigon looked like. Primitive by today's standards, but perfect for black and white. Everyone seemed happy except for one gentleman who informed me that he'd lived in Saigon for 30 years but never seen a bar like it... My stomach turned. I went back to my office feeling very low. Hans was doing his rounds – boy, did he keep track of what everyone was doing – and when he saw me, he asked "what's the problem?" When I told him what had happened, he said, "I

1

2

3

4

6

7

8

5

9

(1–9) **To Kill a Mockingbird**: As part of his research for the film, Bumstead scouted the novel's Alabama settings with its author Harper Lee. (1) From the plans he subsequently drew up of the main exterior street set, his assistant Dale Hennessey created the production sketch. (3–4, 6–8) Storyboards for sequences shot on the set. "When the picture was released, I received calls from top art directors at other studios wanting to know where in Alabama we'd shot the film. I'd reply, 'It was all done on the back-lot' and they'd laugh and say, 'No, really, Bummy. Where?' So then I began to realise, well, I guess it's a pretty good job."

want you to go right back to the stage, get ahold of this so-called technical adviser, and ask him if he's seen every bar in Saigon. And he'll say, 'well, no, but I've seen most of 'em.' And then you just tell him, well, you missed this one – it was just around the corner." Sure enough, after I'd taken this advice, I never heard another peep from the adviser. The second lesson I learned from Hans was on another picture where I had to design a guy's apartment. I was short of money, so I decided to have it dressed from stock units, and I found three beautiful book cases. When Hans saw the set, he said: "The owner of this apartment, he's a very learned man, isn't he?" And he walked out. I was bemused. I thought about it, and realised that, no, he wasn't learned at all, he probably never reads. And that's what Hans was driving at. From that day, I began to think in terms of character when I designed. I don't try to show every colour or every design trick I know. I try to tailor everything to the character. Take Scottie Ferguson in **Vertigo**. An ex-cop, probably not a great reader. I made him a philatelist, and dressed a corner of his living room with stamp magazines, magnifying glass and all the equipment a stamp collector uses. That's the kind of detail Hitchcock loved to see.

Once I'm on a picture, I get lost in it. I think about it night and day. When I begin to design, I read the script maybe two or three times. Then I try to visualise it, so by the time I'm doodling my rough sketches, I know exactly in my mind how it should look. I do a lot of my designing riding to and from the studio. When I was starting out, I worked with Michael Curtiz, and I made the mistake of explaining to him how to

pan across a set. "Don't you tell me where to pan," he replied, "I was doing pictures before you were in diapers." But how you stage the action is as much the designer's concern as the director's. Where are the characters' entrances and exits? Where are they going to stand or sit? How close should the sofa be to the fireplace? You can't lay out a set or pick a location if you don't have that understanding. Clint Eastwood embarrasses me by arriving on set and saying, "Well, Bummy, where do you want me to put the camera?"

Most directors I've worked with leave the design decisions to me. Even with someone like Hitch (who started in the industry as an art director), there'd be three things in the picture he'd want, and the rest would be up to me, right down to picking the locations. By discussing the set dressing, painting, ageing and special requirements the director may have in advance, it saves a lot of time and money during production. But knowing how – and when – to talk to the director is essential. At Paramount, if I wanted to get Hitch to okay a set, I'd always check with his assistant to see if he was in a good mood. If so, I'd show him. If not, I'd wait. When I was an assistant art director, I once worked for an art director who just steamed into a rehearsal, spun the director around and told him, "hey, I have to sign off on this set". Well, the director went to the phone and told the production office, "I don't want to see that guy on my set again."

When I'm breaking a script down, one of the most important factors is deciding what should be done in the studio and what should be location. When I started working on **The**

(1–10) **Unforgiven**: After Bumstead and Clint Eastwood found the location near Calgary for Big Whiskey (3), the designer returned to L.A. and spent three weeks designing the exterior street set, which was then built and dressed in just 38 days. (1) Rough model of the set to aid the construction department's carpenters and (2) aerial photograph of the set, which was built for ease of shooting on an east-west axis. (4–9) Big Whiskey during and after construction: the tight schedule meant that the design had to be kept simple.

1

2

3

4

5

(1–5) **Unforgiven**: (2–3) The interior of adobe house belonging to Bill Munny (Eastwood) built on location in Brooks, Canada: "A difficult set to build, because the carpenters we hired in Canada weren't used to doing character-driven sets." (4–5) Construction of Munny's pig farm.

Sting for George Roy Hill, I'd heard that it was hard to find a full street in Chicago (the film's setting) which didn't have modern buildings, signage or street-lighting. So I told George we should shoot the film on the lot. Well, he blew his top: "I hate the goddam lot!" So we went to Chicago and picked a few things out, but after the shoot, George came up to me and said, "you know, the best-looking stuff on this picture is what we shot on the lot." Hitch preferred the comfort of the studio. He liked to get out of his car and walk two or three steps to his director's chair. On **Family Plot**, he turned up for a location night shoot after a good supper. The window of his limousine was wound down (I was nearly asphyxiated by the smell of cognac and cigar smoke) and he said, "Can't we do this back at the studio? How do you expect me to get a performance out of my actors and actresses in this cold?" The night shoot was cancelled; we built the set on the stage at Universal... But the beauty of shooting in the studio is that you can design everything; you're really able to play with the space and have some fun with it. On location, there's only so much latitude you have.

I always try to soak up the mood of a picture. That's why doing the research is such a wonderful time. What you're looking for with research is a trigger. For **The Sting**, I was influenced by Walker Evans' pictures from The Depression era. Often, it's not so specific. You might get inspiration from a picture of a room in a magazine – even if it's not the right style, there may be something in the layout of the space that gives you a spark. Unfortunately, with today's tight schedules, it's almost impossible to have enough time for research. On **Midnight in the Garden of Good and Evil**, I was one jump ahead of the sheriff – we had one month to prepare the whole picture. With **Unforgiven** we had 38 days to build the entire western town. The schedule forced me to keep the design simple. Ultimately, however, that simplicity set the tone for the entire picture and every actor came up to thank us for our work. It's so important to create a mood for the cast through the set design. It really helps them with their performances.

Whenever I've had to design a western street, I've always run it from east to west, to give the cameraman the possibility of using backlight at the beginning and end of the day. I always think of what I'm giving the cameraman in terms of opportunities for coverage, and ease of shooting. All my walls in **Unforgiven** were "wild". Just as a good cameraman can make me look good, I can make them look good in turn. I remember a screenwriter once saying to me, "colour can make even the garbage cans in an alley look beautiful", so I'm very discriminating about how I use colour. But I'll always consult with the cameraman, and the costume designer. Movie-making is about collaboration. When everyone's work gels, you know you've got a good picture on your hands. I've been lucky in my career. I've worked steady. I've had good directors and good scripts. I've had a fantastic life – travelled all over the world, met wonderful people. I love it. I guess that's why I'm still working at 84. If there's any advice I'd pass on, it would be to observe. Observe everything. Especially details like ageing. Nowadays, people don't know how a fireplace ages (it's white at the bottom). Observation is the key ability to cultivate.

biography

It should come as no surprise to anyone who has been awed by Ken Adam's flying cars, rockets, airships and space-stations that this bold visionary of film design began adult life as a fighter pilot in the RAF, or that he describes himself as a "sports-car fiend". Adam's work has had a profound influence not just on his profession but on the whole look of modern film. He is responsible for the larger-than-life, but tongue-in-

ken adam

cheek tone and style of the James Bond films: he designed **Dr No** (1962), **Goldfinger** (1964), **Thunderball** (1965), **You Only Live Twice** (1967), **Diamonds are Forever** (1971), **The Spy Who Loved Me** (1977) and **Moonraker** (1979). Stanley Kubrick, recognising the design genius of the early Bonds, hired Adam for **Dr Strangelove** (1963), which the designer regards as the most important film he has worked on. He collaborated again with Kubrick on **Barry Lyndon** (1974), which together with **The Trials of Oscar Wilde** (1960, Ken Hughes) and **The Madness of King George** (1994, Nicholas Hytner) demonstrates how Adam could apply his vision to period, literary subjects as well as the Bond films and **Dr Strangelove**. It was also harnessed to brilliant effect in **Sleuth** (1972, Joseph Mankiewicz), **Pennies From Heaven** (1981, Herbert Ross) and **Addams Family Values** (1993, Barry Sonnenfeld).

interview

When people ask me what are the essentials of becoming a successful production designer, I always say you need talent and imagination, but you also have to have luck, the courage of your convictions, and the ability to communicate.

Craft came easily to me. From an early age, I was able to draw rather well. Growing up in Berlin during the rise of Nazism, my imagination was fed by German Expressionist cinema like **The Cabinet of Dr Caligari** and also by the ideas and aesthetics of the Bauhaus movement. I knew I wanted to be a designer, but it wasn't until my family had left Germany to settle in England and, aged 15, I met the art director Vincent Korda, that I set my mind on film. I followed Korda's advice to study architecture first, and when I eventually entered the industry after the war, first as a junior draughtsman, then as an assistant art director, this background gave me a knowledge of different period styles and made it easy for me to provide a functional, acceptable set. However, I found it dull merely to imitate reality. I was never satisfied with playing safe. I instinctively gravitated towards a more theatrical approach which gave free rein to my imagination.

I was enormously lucky to work for a time during the 1940s and '50s with Georges Wakhévitch, the Russian designer. Although he had designed films like **La Grande Illusion** for Renoir, he was perhaps better known for his work in opera and theatre. A stage designer has to create a self-sufficient universe within the proscenium arch and the dimensions of the stage. These limits mean that one cannot simply reproduce reality; one is much more dependent on imagination. I began to realise that this approach could be applied to film. I experimented with theatrical stylisation on **Around the World in 80 Days**, whose associate producer was William Cameron Menzies, the father of modern production design. Menzies encouraged me to stylise, and he taught me not to be afraid to use colour in bold ways. But it was practical considerations as much as aesthetic ideals that forced me to apply these ideas to **The Trials of Oscar Wilde**. The low art department budget meant I could not have attempted authentic period reproductions even if I wanted to. I had to simplify the design – and this led to a stylisation for which I won critical recognition for the first time.

This approach has sustained me for the past 50 years, but it should be said that although I am interested in heightening a film's visual impact, it is never stylisation for stylisation's sake. My aim has been to create a stylised reality for the audience that in the context of a particular dramatic moment or character is more "real" than a literal interpretation of reality. To some degree, the Bond films are a good example. When **Goldfinger** was released, we received letters from people demanding to know how we had obtained permission to enter Fort Knox when even the President of the United States wasn't allowed inside. The truth was we hadn't. I was allowed to recce the exterior, which we reproduced on the lot at Pinewood studios, but the interior was complete invention. In reality, gold is too heavy to be stacked in the way I depicted, but I felt that an audience being taken into the world's biggest bullion deposit would want to see towers of gold 40-feet high.

As I said, a designer needs luck as well as talent and imagination. I was especially lucky when I designed the first Bond film, **Dr No**. The director Terence Young (who saw himself as a Bond figure, and was responsible for grooming Sean Connery in the role) left the design of the sets totally in my hands while he shot on location in Jamaica. As I filled five of Pinewood's stages with sets, it was the first time I was really able to let my imagination go. I was fascinated by the possibility of creating interiors like Dr No's apartment and the nuclear reactor. I called together all the heads of department at Pinewood, and told them that I wanted to experiment with new materials; I wanted to move away from the old techniques and traditional methods of film design. For example, in the past, a flat would be covered with hessian, then with paper, before the painters went to work on it to create a paint effect according to the type of finish required: a labour-intensive, costly process (it's easy to forget that **Dr No** was a low-budget

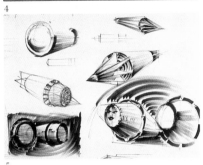

(1–7) **Dr Strangelove**: (7) Ken Adam in his War-Room set. Stanley Kubrick vetoed his original design (1) because of the cost of having to fill the upper gallery with extras. Adam went back to the drawing-board and metaphorical associations with gambling and bomb shelters yielded the final design (6). Kubrick wanted only source lighting on the set so Adam designed the circular light fitting suspended over the table (3). Sketches of the B52 bomber and bombs (4–5).

ken adam

1

28

3

5

2

4

6

7

(1–10) The James Bond films gave full rein to Adam's imagination while remaining "very linear, with a simplicity of line". He used modern technology and new building materials and finishes to create Bond's world. (7) The lair in **Dr No** for which Adam painted a reproduction of a Goya portrait which – in real life – had recently been stolen from London's National Gallery and whose fictional reappearance on Dr No's wall left audiences in 1962 in no doubt about his criminal credentials. **Goldfinger**: (1–2) Fort Knox; (3–4) the rumpus room; (5–6) laser beam interrogation chamber ("Do you expect me to talk?" "No, Mister Bond, I expect you to die").

The Bond films reflected Adam's Bauhaus inspiration and his love of expressionistic and futuristic films such as **Metropolis** and **Things to Come**. These influences are apparent in the volcano interior set for **You Only Live Twice** (8–10), in 1967 the most ambitious set ever built in Europe. "It was such a tall structure, and its odd shape meant that it had to be constructed as a free-standing set [rather than on a studio stage]. It was built to be shot from the inside only."

(1) **The Spy Who Loved Me** required the largest soundstage in the world to be constructed at Pinewood Studios to house the interior of the villain's nuclear submarine-gobbling supertanker. (2) **Thunderball** M's conference room in London. (3–4) SPECTRE's conference room in Paris. (5–7) **Moonraker** space station interior.

film; the art department budget was £21,000). I had heard of a new process in which nitric acid was sprayed on to the surface until it became like a mirror, on top of which you could then spray lacquer – copper, brass, stainless steel. We combined these metallic surfaces with ply veneered in every type of wood finish – and these new materials actually enabled us to save money. Of equal importance, the fact that we were embarking on such a big challenge and using new methods excited the whole team. In my experience, whenever your department is involved in something they think is out of the ordinary, there's a sense of excitement that is infectious which makes everyone rise to the challenge.

The volcano set I designed for **You Only Live Twice** is a good example of another valuable attribute required to be a successful production designer. You have to have the courage of your convictions – and the more far-fetched your conviction is, the more courage you need. By 1967, the Bond series had become unbelievably successful. **You Only Live Twice** was already booked into 4,000 cinemas – before we even had a workable script. Moreover, time was running out on Sean's contract. Despite extensive recces in Japan, we had failed to find the locations described in Fleming's book. Near the end of the trip, we were in the helicopter flying over the Kyushu volcano region, and we began to improvise ideas: wouldn't it be interesting to have the villain inside one of these extinct craters? I started to sketch. Cubby Broccoli, one of the producers, asked, "How much is it going to cost?" Well, it cost $1m, it was the most expensive free-standing set ever built; but then it couldn't be equated with normal film design,

because something on this scale (120-feet high, 400 feet in diameter, with a 70-foot diameter sliding-door set at an angle at the top, requiring 700 tons of structural steel) becomes as much an engineering as a design challenge. I tried to cover myself by calling in structural engineers, but it was still a huge experiment. I knew my career was on the line. If it didn't work out, I'd never work again. No wonder I broke out in eczema. But as soon as the crew saw the structure begin to emerge, they became so enthusiastic that they were virtually willing to risk their lives to achieve it.

The ability to communicate is an essential skill to cultivate. All the key personnel on a film are invariably people with big egos, but they have to co-exist in harmony if the collaboration is to succeed. On **Dr No** I was lucky that I was able to create the sets without anyone looking over my shoulder. Working with Stanley Kubrick was a very different proposition – but **Dr Strangelove** proved a vital step in my development as a production designer. Kubrick was a brilliant visual director, and although we hit it off, he was extremely difficult and demanding to work for. When we met to discuss the War-Room set, I scribbled a two-level set which he immediately said he liked. I thought, well, that was easy; and the art department began to draw up plans and build models. One morning, three weeks later (when work on the set was well advanced), I was giving Stanley a lift to Shepperton, when he turned to me and said, "About the War-Room, Ken... I don't think the two-level concept will work; what am I going to do with the upper level? It's too costly to fill it with extras..." Well, this threw me. I went into tailspin. I walked around the

(1–2) Chocolate factory in **Chitty Chitty Bang Bang** shows the influence of German Expressionism on Adam's work. Painters such as Reginald Marsh and Edward Hopper and photographer Walker Evans were important influences on the period look of **Pennies From Heaven** (3–15), which was shot entirely in the studio at MGM. The story contrasts the grim reality of Chicago during The Depression with the hero and heroine's escapist fantasies based on Hollywood musicals. (3) Preparatory scene painting (with model out of focus in foreground) for "el street" set. (4–5) Interior of the bank, for which Adam used art deco styling to create "a marble cathedral to money". (6–7) Interior of the bar. (8–9) Exterior of the diner. (10–11) Interior of the flop house. (12–13) Exterior of the movie theatre and (14–15) model and conceptual sketch for "el street" set.

4

5

6

7

8

9

10

11

12

13

14

15

production design & art direction

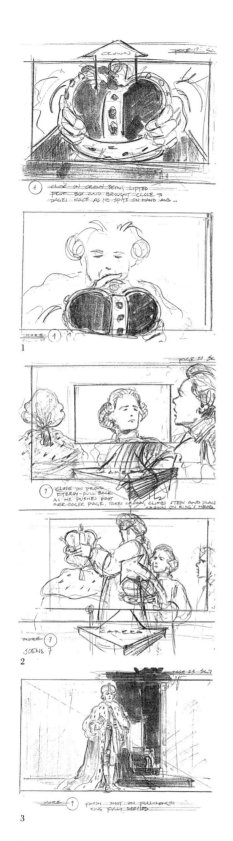

1

2

3

4

5

6

(1–12) **The Madness of King George**: Adam urged stage director Nicholas Hytner to use his flair for theatricality on the film adaptation of Alan Bennett's play 'The Madness of King George': "I will give you theatrical backgrounds, but with the space you never had for the theatre production." (1–3) Storyboard for opening of film. (4) Illustration for nursery interior and (5) illustration for the King's bedroom.

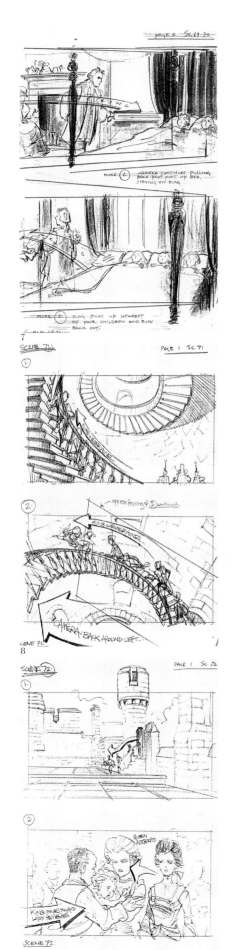

(7–9) Storyboard for sequence dramatising the height of George's madness. Spiral staircase shot in St Paul's Cathedral; rooftop shot at Arundel Castle (12). Adam added extra chimneys to evoke the stylised atmosphere of a Greek tragedy. (10) Illustration, Prince of Wales dining room. (11) Illustration, Kew House – for the scenes in this set where the King is treated for his madness, Adam stripped the interior of almost all furnishings, creating the feeling of a prison within the perfectly proportioned interior.

(1–7) **Addams Family Values**: Adam believes that the sketch is the designer's most important tool. To obtain a sense of chiaroscuro (light/shadow) and the feeling of the set's mass and scale, he always starts the design process with black and white thumbnail sketches, before proceeding to more detailed colour renderings, scale plans or models.

garden at Shepperton for over an hour trying to calm myself down. Then I began scribbling again – with Stanley looking over my shoulder. I doodled various shapes before coming up with a triangular form. Stanley stopped me. "Isn't the triangle the strongest form in geometry?" he asked. Me: "You may well be right." Him: "In other words, it would make for a good bomb shelter." Me: "Reinforced concrete." Him: "A huge, underground bomb shelter – fantastic." I elaborated on the design with big maps and a circular table. Him: "Green baize on the table..." Me: "...The film's in black and white." Him: "Yeah, but the table, it's like the President and his generals all taking part in a gigantic poker game." And that's how the concept was born. I have it on very good authority that when Ronald Reagan became President he asked his Chief-of-Staff if he could be shown the War-Room.

As a designer, one is dependent on others to make one's concepts actually work in practice. On the Bond films, I was also fortunate enough to have a team of some of the best technicians working in England at the time. John Stears – who did the special effects – and I worked very closely to create gadgets such as the Aston Martin DB5. Surrounding yourself with good people is essential – a wonderful set dresser will bring things to a set you might not even have thought of – but it's important that everyone operates within the overall design style, just as the designer must bear in mind that the design should serve the film. I was fortunate to work twice with Laurence Olivier, an actor who paid enormous attention to his props and how he interacted with his surroundings. On the set of **Sleuth**, I remember he decided to play an entire scene from a position by the fireplace I'd designed. As I watched him rehearse, my attention was distracted by three props on the mantle. I sneaked up and removed them. After we'd shot the scene, Olivier said to me, "I'm glad you did that. I knew they wouldn't fit in." I've probably been guilty of designing sets which overpower the actors on some of the Bonds, but ultimately I believe that the designer should think of a set as a frame for the actor to work in.

biography

Sylbert has collaborated with some of the finest post-war American directors: Elia Kazan (**Baby Doll**, 1956; **A Face in the Crowd**, 1957; **Splendor in the Grass**, 1961), Sidney Lumet (**Long Day's Journey Into Night**, 1962; **The Pawnbroker**, 1964), John Frankenheimer (**The Manchurian Candidate**, 1962), Mike Nichols (**Who's Afraid of Virginia Woolf?**, 1966; **The Graduate**, 1967;

richard sylbert

Catch 22, 1970; **Carnal Knowledge**, 1971), Roman Polanski (**Rosemary's Baby**, 1968; **Chinatown**, 1974), John Huston (**Fat City**, 1972), Hal Ashby (**Shampoo**, 1975), Warren Beatty (**Reds**, 1981; **Dick Tracy**, 1990) and Francis Ford Coppola (**The Cotton Club**, 1984). He designed **Bonfire of The Vanities** (1990) and **Carlito's Way** (1993) for Brian De Palma, who said of Sylbert: "You give him your ideas, and he gives you back ideas that are better." His approach is built on a bedrock of craft learned as a scenic painter in theatre and television following formal training as a fine artist in New York. Recipient of an Honorary Doctorate of Fine Arts from the American Film Institute in 1992 (as well as two Oscars and four nominations), Sylbert is one of the most influential contemporary production designers. He was vice-president of production at Paramount Studios (1975–78), and also designed the permanent set for *Cheers* in 1982.

interview

If someone says "cinematographer", you think, oh yeah, that's the guy who does the camerawork. "Costume designer" – that's also easy to define. But what is a "production designer"? It's a title searching for a definition. People without any technical ability get Oscars – for renting chateaux in France or stately homes in England (by rights, the National Trust should have more Oscars than many production designers working today). Giving an award to a "production designer" who rents buildings is as nonsensical as nominating a cinematographer for available-light photography (although that happens, too). To me, that isn't what production design is about. When I began working in the industry, you made all the illustrations, you drew up the plans, you decorated the sets, you picked all the locations. Today, most designers on a big production will have dozens of people working for them. The most I've ever had (even on a picture like **Dick Tracy**) is six. Imagine Mozart saying to somebody, "I have a great idea for a piece of music, but I don't know how to play the piano.

I'll hum it for you." The fact is, Mozart was the finest pianist of his day, just as Michelangelo was the greatest marble carver. Most production designers today are hummers. They have ideas, get all the research together, but can't draw up a $^1/_4$-inch plan. They have no idea how to commit to details – where to put windows or doors, how to create mouldings or age a wall.

The first and greatest production designer was William Cameron Menzies. In 1950, he directed the first movie I designed – a Fu Manchu story. Every evening we'd meet up; he'd make sketches of the shots he wanted on the hotel stationery. And as we talked, I learned about what a production designer did, from the man for whom the title was invented. It's important to understand what Menzies achieved. He was brought to Hollywood by Douglas Fairbanks Snr in 1919 as an illustrator. He'd make an illustration for, say, **The Thief of Baghdad**. The illustration would be painted on glass so that they could check that the finished set matched what he'd drawn. He worked for journeyman directors like Sam Wood who wouldn't have known where to put the camera without Menzies' illustrations. Aged 20, he won his first Academy Award as art director. What he did was to structure a film's visual content. Such was his input on **Gone with the Wind**, that Selznick created the title "production designer" for him. Every shot was based on his storyboards, and the whole picture was made without leaving the confines of the studio. That's production design.

The storyboard was Menzies' primary tool to control how a picture looked, but for the directors I found myself working with in the 1950s – people like Elia Kazan, Sidney Lumet, Martin Ritt – such a method had no relevance. What the hell would Kazan want with a storyboard? – He's waiting for the actor to get into the room. He's not interested in the camera set-up, he's interested in what the actor is doing. Like all the greatest directors I've worked with, Kazan fits the model of Homer – the blind storyteller. His overriding concern was with the emotional dynamics of the narrative. As a designer, I had to figure out ways other than storyboarding to achieve Menzies' goal of visual control. I'd listen to Kazan talking about the script; he sought out what was beyond the text, around the text, below the text, behind the text – in search of the basic action of the story. He talked in metaphors. The Loomis house in **Splendor in the Grass** "should feel like a homey stew," he'd tell me. "Comforting, warm." Metaphor. Basic action. Emotional dynamics. These became the keys to the approach I evolved over the years. My aim is to rewrite a script in visual terms; to reflect dramatic structure through the design elements at my disposal – architectural space, line, colour, pattern, repetition, contrast. I write a "recipe" for the design of each film I work on. Take **Chinatown**, whose basic action is summed up in a line of dialogue: "Find the girl". The setting is L.A. in 1937 during a drought. That means there cannot be any water, except in certain specific places where it has dramatic meaning (e.g. the pond in Mrs Mulwray's garden, or the illegally-irrigated orange grove). There cannot be any clouds in the sky (if there were, it would be liable to rain). The colour palette must evoke heat and the absence of water. The spectrum in the film thus starts with the

(1–5) **Chinatown**: (1) Art department illustration (by Joe Hurley) of Ida Sessions' house. Based on Sylbert's location photograph, it illustrates key ingredients of the film's design "recipe" – white, Spanish colonial façade evoking heat, cloudless blue sky intimating drought. Sylbert also picked this location for its neat symmetry (everything is stable) punctuated by the narrow corridor. The theme of drought is subliminally evoked elsewhere in (2) the frosted glass of office doors, (4) the parched Californian desert landscape. (5) The film's poster was based on the logo Sylbert created for the production.

production design & art direction

(1–2) **Carnal Knowledge**: Art department illustrations convey Sylbert's design concept: "There is a) nothing on the walls of any set and b) in every set outside any window there is another window." (3) **The Graduate**: The two family homes were designed to mirror and counterpoint each other according to the principle of "keeping up with the Joneses".

colour of "burnt grass" (actually the name of a wallpaper design I picked out for a set) and goes through umber, white, straw yellow, to a brown the shade of peanut butter. Every building we see must reflect the Spanish colonial style, not just because it's right for the period, but also because such architecture is white. And white makes you feel hotter. To get anywhere, the detective must be made to walk or drive uphill. It's harder work for him that way (especially in the heat). The highest point we see will be Evelyn Mulwray's home, which is surrounded by sky. In the one instance when the detective does go downhill, again it's for a dramatic reason. He descends into a ravine where there's no water – the scene offers a key to the political conspiracy at the heart of the story. The theme of water is also repeated in the glass sections of office doors: they are opaque, suggesting mystery – you can't see clearly what's happening on the other side. They also make you think of frozen water. I've learned about repetition from music: in classical sonata form, a theme may be repeated in a number of different keys, each time adding a different resonance. In **Chinatown**, certain sets are designed to echo others, for example the Water and Power Department and the police morgue are deliberately reminiscent of each other in terms of colour and geography. One last ingredient: symmetry – used to create a sense of false security. For the scene where the detective visits Ida Sessions' house, I found a building with perfectly symmetrical lines – look how nice and balanced it is, everything's fine here... Then you see broken glass and realise the woman inside has been murdered.

If I didn't think like this, I'd be painting by numbers, faithfully reproducing the sets called for by the script. Having a recipe not only gives me visual control over the film's design, it also helps me to navigate the tortuous production process, where everything is shot out of sequence. **Reds**, for example, required 150 sets and took two years to make, but when you looked closely at the story, it had a relatively simple structure – like a 19th-century symphonic poem. You went from America to Russia back to America back to Russia. Like a piece of music which attempts to return to the "home" key at the end, the script finished with John Reed dying in Russia, and the last thing he says is, "Well, I'm ready to go home" (followed by a coda featuring the songs of his childhood). The key to the design was the contrast between the two countries; everything in America was depicted as being small in scale, cramped. In Russia, where the characters were like innocents abroad, everything was immense, presented on an epic scale. We also rigorously controlled the colour throughout the film. The idea was to "protect" the flag: the red in both the Russian and American flags was the key colour to represent. D.P. Vittorio Storaro and I gravitated to a look inspired by tonal painting and Lewis Mumphet's reference to the period as "the brown decades". If **Reds** was a symphonic poem, **Carnal Knowledge** was a piece of contemporary chamber music. Mike Nichols and I talked about **Jules et Jim**, specifically the way Truffaut drove the actors into the corners of rooms, literally "cornering" them. We pushed this approach a step further. Every door in every room you see is in a corner. And every window looks out on to another window, endlessly repeating the action that's being played out (when we shot a night exterior in Park

richard sylbert

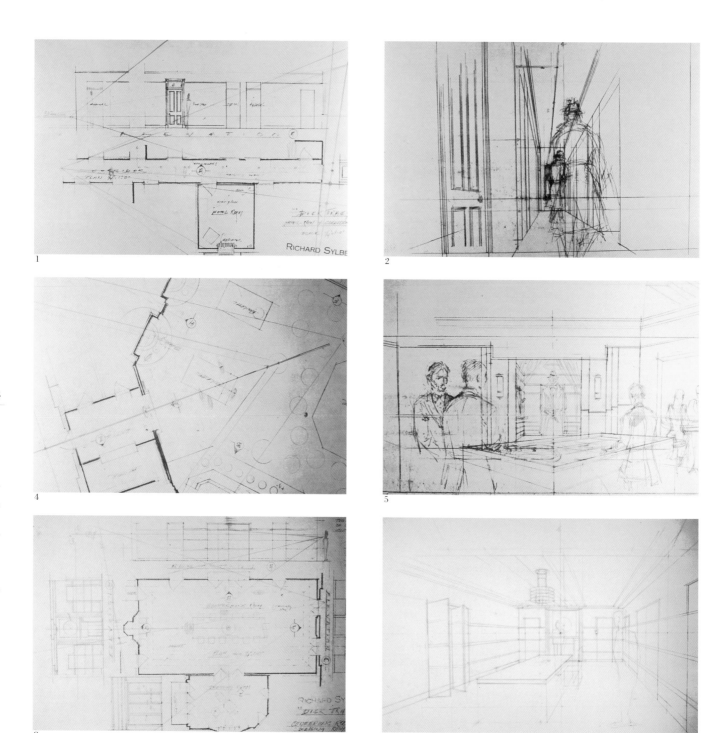

1

2

RICHARD SYLBE

4

5

8

9

12

13

14

16

6

7

11

10

15

(1–16) **Dick Tracy**: Sylbert's design process is exemplified by plans and drawings made for three studio sets (1–11). He first draws ¼-inch plans and elevations, from which he makes a projected drawing of an establishing view of the set. This is then turned over to an illustrator along with specifications for colour. Sylbert also produces conceptual drawings for scenes which will combine sets and matte paintings: (12–13) the graveyard and (14–15) cityscape.

1

production design & art direction

2

(1) When designing the nightclub for **Carlito's Way**, Sylbert used the metaphor of a ship that never sails to embody the idea of the protagonists' thwarted desire to escape. The illustrations for **Mobsters** ("a wonderful-looking bad movie" says the designer) show (2) Sylbert's conceptual drawing of a 1920s' New York street scene (for a scene combining set construction and matte painting) and (3) matte painter Leon Harris' final version.

3

Avenue, we were able to make people turn on their lights to emphasise the windows). I wanted the film to have the quality of a dream or of memory, so I deliberately left the walls in all the rooms in the film bare. There's nothing there except for the light fixtures, until the last scene of the film where there is a photograph of "her", the girl.

Who's Afraid of Virginia Woolf? represented the other extreme to this deliberately sparse approach. It was a film about two pack-rats, academics who go off travelling on sabbaticals and whose house is full of clutter they've collected through the years. I selected every book, every postcard, every item and dressed it into the set. I find contemporary movies more difficult and more challenging than period films; you have less to start with, you really have to dig deep for the design ideas. For **Shampoo**, I spent a lot of time researching the world of beauty parlours before the right metaphorical idea hit me: to represent Beverly Hills as a modern garden of earthly delights. Lattice-work became a visual leitmotif, repeated throughout the picture in different locations. I also took the central idea of social climbing and visualised it by having the characters live on different levels according to their social status. The hairdresser Warren Beatty is at the bottom of the Hills; Goldie Hawn is halfway up; the serious money is at the top, where Jack Warden lives in a house with $8m-worth of art on the walls. The more socially elevated characters could literally look down on their inferiors. The key to **The Graduate**, another project with a contemporary setting, was found by thinking about how to represent the two families. Initially I played with the notion of depicting them like Capulets and Montagues, two powerful families at each other's throats. But this idea wasn't true to Buck Henry's screenplay. They were, in fact, the same kind of family, living on the same street with the same values and the same ideas. So, I found two identical houses on a street and then I designed interiors so that they would resonate with each other, for example by reversing the blacks and whites in each home. Where the staircase in Dustin Hoffmann's home has a white balustrade, Katherine Ross's home has a black one. And where his house features square lines, all the openings in her's are rounded. Everything is echoed, except the design of Mrs Robinson's bedroom. She's a predator, she wears leopard skin. The jungle is the metaphor for her environment.

Making movies used to be fun. Now, unhappily, the fun has been surgically removed by the suits with MBAs who micro-manage film production. You spend more time trying to reduce a budget than you do thinking about the film, and then the picture gets cancelled because the stars aren't available. These days it seems there are 200 executives and four actors. It used to be the other way around. This trend has been accompanied by the rise of directors schooled in MTV and commercials, catering for audiences with ever-decreasing attention spans (somebody recently told me they'd seen **Chinatown** again: "Gosh, it's a slow movie.") Their visual pyrotechnics negate the production designer's creative role – but still more troubling is the fact that the movies they make have no real core. They are about nothing. If you want to find a worthwhile movie to watch today, you're in real trouble.

biography

A dedicated film-lover from early childhood, Ferretti studied at the Academy of Fine Arts in Rome in the early 1960s, while moon-lighting as an assistant art director. Two directors were to prove the formative influences on his career – Pier Paolo Pasolini and Federico Fellini. For Pasolini, he designed **Medea** (1970), **The Decameron** (1970), **The Canterbury Tales** (1971), **Arabian Nights** (1974) and **The 120 Days**

dante ferretti

of Sodom (1975); for Fellini, **An Orchestra Rehearsal** (1978), **City of Women** (1980), **And the Ship Sails On** (1983), **Ginger and Fred** (1986) and **The Voice of the Moon** (1990). While based at Cinecittà Studios, Ferretti also designed two epic American productions, **The Name of the Rose** (1986, Jean-Jacques Annaud) and **The Adventures Of Baron Munchausen** (1988, Terry Gilliam). His international career flourished: he designed **Hamlet** (1990) for Franco Zeffirelli, before beginning a collaboration with Martin Scorsese with **The Age of Innocence** (1993) followed by **Casino** (1995), **Kundun** (1997) and **Bringing out the Dead** (1999). He has also designed **Interview with the Vampire** (1994, Neil Jordan), **Meet Joe Black** (1998, Martin Brest) and **Titus** (1999, Julie Taymor). As well as his work in film, he is renowned for his opera design.

interview

I was born to be a production designer. Aged 13, I'd go to see **Ben-Hur** or **Quo Vadis** and dream of building the scenery for such movies, just as someone else might dream of acting in them. I studied fine art and architecture and served my apprenticeship in the art department on Italian B (and C and D) movies for eight years; but it was when I began to work as a designer for Pasolini and Fellini that I really learned about making movies. They were two completely different personalities. I was always a little intimidated by Pasolini. He was like a poet or a priest, and his approach to film-making was architectural: his shots were always like geometrical tableaux, with the camera dead centre. He worked from the head. Fellini worked from the heart. We both grew up around Rimini so we shared the same mentality, the same humour. But you didn't work with Fellini, you worked for him. You were the servant of his dreams. He really got inside your head – you had to live and breathe Fellini. He was very possessive, and could behave like a jilted lover if you left to work with

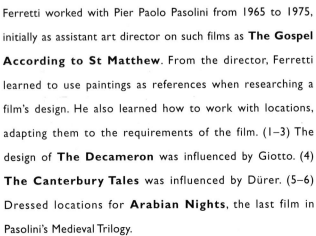

Ferretti worked with Pier Paolo Pasolini from 1965 to 1975, initially as assistant art director on such films as **The Gospel According to St Matthew**. From the director, Ferretti learned to use paintings as references when researching a film's design. He also learned how to work with locations, adapting them to the requirements of the film. (1–3) The design of **The Decameron** was influenced by Giotto. (4) **The Canterbury Tales** was influenced by Dürer. (5–6) Dressed locations for **Arabian Nights**, the last film in Pasolini's Medieval Trilogy.

other directors. When he first asked me to design a movie for him, I was 25. I said, "No. I can't." The reason was that I was scared of being fired by him – I had worked on **Satyricon** as an art director and seen him fire everyone else in the art department. I didn't want my career to be destroyed while I was still trying to establish myself. So I told him, "call me in ten years' time". Years later, we bumped into each other one night at Cinecittà Studios in Rome under a street light. He insisted ten years had passed; in fact it was more like eight, but by then I was ready... With Fellini, every design idea was born out of the two of us talking together. I'd do a sketch, for example, and he would add an idea that gave it another dimension. It was a process of continuous improvisation. Fellini taught me that in the cinema, everything is possible. Whereas Pasolini's style was a form of poetic naturalism, Fellini's was pure fantasy.

With Pasolini, all the research we did came from looking at paintings. I have continued this way of working throughout my career. When an artist paints a picture, he creates his own reality which is very different to a faithful reproduction of what he sees. He selects a point of focus and leaves out all the irrelevant details. This is my philosophy when I design a film. I always try to find ways of manipulating reality to accentuate the central focus. I'll exaggerate certain details and discard others. Pasolini also taught me a great lesson about how to work with reality. On **The Decameron**, he wanted to feature an architectural detail which I knew was a century later than the film's Renaissance setting. When I questioned him about it, he replied: "Don't worry, we are predicting the future."

This made me rethink my whole approach. Now I'm not so worried about being completely authentic; I'm more concerned with getting the right feeling in what I do.

Fellini taught me another invaluable lesson about how to handle realism. Near the beginning of our collaboration, I designed a set which featured a sink. For the sake of realism, I drew all the details around the basin – the taps, and all the pipe work. As soon as Fellini saw my drawing, he said, "lose the pipes". He thought of films as dreams, and he reasoned that when one has a dream, it's never like reality. One only "sees" what is essential to the action of the dream. In the case of my set, the sink was essential but the pipes were not. They would take you out of the dream and return you to reality. Fellini loved to play with reality. Everything on our sets was exaggerated or distorted – not just in the set design, but also in the furnishings and props: a chair was never a normal chair, but always a little bit too big.

However, although Fellini and Pasolini taught me to be flexible with reality, I don't like losing all sense of it because otherwise the audience doesn't believe what you show them. **The Adventures of Baron Munchausen** was different – you could justify putting cake on the moon, for example, because the whole story was being fabricated by a compulsive liar and a seven-year-old child. Archaeological fantasy is perhaps the best way to define my approach. There's always an archaeological aspect to production design, even if the period setting is very recent. **Casino** was set in the 1970s, but there's nothing left from the period in contemporary Las

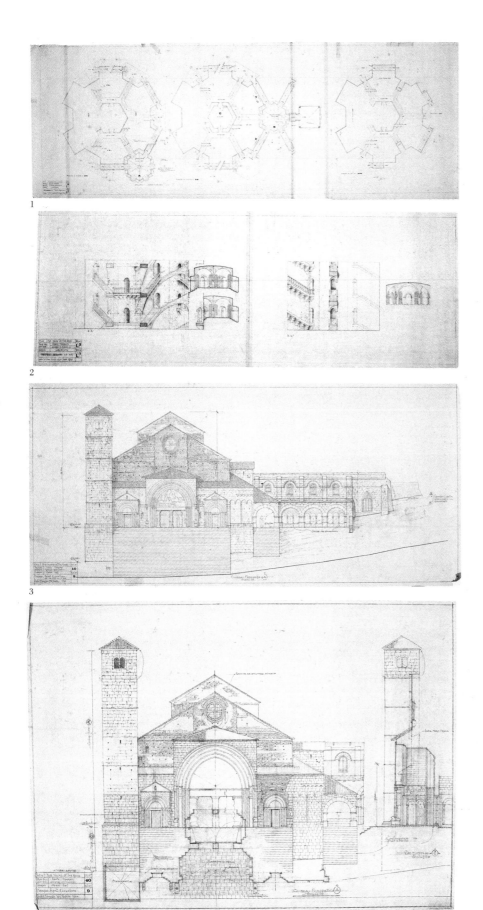

1

2

3

4

5

6

7

8

11

9

12

10

13

(1–13) **The Name of the Rose**: "I was very inspired by the atmosphere of Umberto Eco's novel. It really evoked the Dark Ages. I wanted to give the film's design a subterranean, mysterious quality." (1–2) Plans and sections for the Escher-inspired labyrinth set: "How do you give the feeling of a labyrinth on film? If it's designed horizontally, it's difficult to tell that it's a labyrinth, but if you do it vertically, then you really get a sense of it." (3–4) Elevations of the abbey, built on location outside Rome (11–13). Interiors were built at Cinecittà Studios. (8) The manuscript room and (9–10) the trial.

Vegas. Everything had to be recreated. We built on location and added computer-generated backgrounds where necessary. I researched the film by looking at magazines and photographs and reading about it in books, but Martin Scorsese also encouraged me to use my own fantasy.

Perhaps because I am small in stature, I always think on a big scale. However, apart from this compulsion, I don't feel I have a recognisable style. Even if you compare two of my films which are set in the same period – **The Decameron** and **The Name of the Rose** – they look totally different to one another. When I begin to design a film, I have no preconceived notions or preferences, I'm completely free; the style depends on each individual film. But once established, the style of the film cannot jump from one thing to another. **Interview with the Vampire**, for example, takes place in several periods and locations, but I was very careful to maintain an overall visual continuity, while seeking to characterise subtly the individual settings. For example, I changed the colour palette from Afro-American/Caribbean colours for New Orleans (redolent of the swamps, the heat, the humidity) to darker, greyer tones for the scenes in Paris.

Each film has a different style, but for me the design process is always the same. After I've read the script, I like to visit the location to get a sense of how I'm going to have to adapt it, and decide how much can be built there and how much needs to be built in the studio. Then I start to look at references from painting and think about what I have to do. Now I begin to sketch. I work in pastels on a dark paper because it helps

me to emphasise the lighting. My art department then makes technical drawings, from which we subsequently build models. I always make models; if you don't, it's possible that the director can arrive on set and be taken by surprise because he has misinterpreted the drawing. A three-dimensional model allows the director to see exactly how the set will be and you can discuss it and make changes if necessary. It also allows the director to think about how he is going to stage a scene. Once the model is accepted, I build the set and then I dress it. If one has a clear concept for the film and one is on the same wavelength as the director, it's a very simple process.

The director – rather than the script – is always the most important factor when I decide to work on a project. In Italy, I worked with the best directors and if they offered me a project, I never asked to read the script first. Mutual trust is essential between a director and a designer. In America, I've been fortunate to work with Scorsese, not just because for me he is a hero, but because he trusts me so much. He gives me great freedom as a designer.

I have no interest in doing movies which depend only on using existing locations. Why use a production designer to choose locations when you can hire a location manager? What I enjoy is to build on location and adapt it to the aesthetic requirements of the film, which is how I always worked with Pasolini. The experience taught me how to select locations and use them creatively. On **The Adventures of Baron Munchausen**, I spent months designing the city which was

1

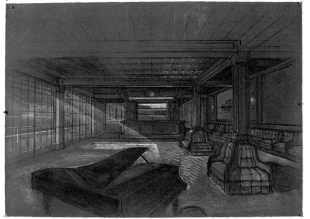

2

5

3

6

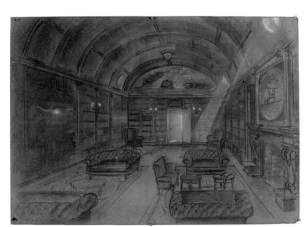

4

7

8

(1–8) "Fellini's **And the Ship Sails On** is my favourite film. It was an incredible challenge: we did the whole film on seven stages in the studio." (1) Harbour set for the Chaplinesque prelude. (2–6) Ocean liner interiors: bar/tearoom (2), the hold (3), library (4), engine room (5) – "I exaggerated the size, as if it was an opera set" – gymnasium (6) and the Austrian battleship (7): Ferretti ultimately opted for one huge cannon in the finished design.

1

2

3

4

5

10

6

8

9

7

(1–10) **The Adventures of Baron Munchausen**: Ferretti abandoned realism to design the flights of fantasy of "the biggest liar who ever lived". His original drawings (1) for the Mediterranean town invaded by the Turks were inspired by Bernardo Bellotto's baroque landscape paintings. When the cost of building it in the studio proved prohibitive, Ferretti remembered a location he had scouted for an aborted project: Belchite, a city bombed during the Spanish Civil War, and untouched ever since. "It was perfect, like a ghost town, with a few baroque and Gothic buildings still standing." (3–4) Belchite served as the foundation for the town sets and invasion scenes. (5–7) In the belly of the giant fish. Ferretti employed specialised craftsmen to build the film's 18th-century ships.

1

2

3

4

5

6

7

8   9   10

(1–10) **Kundun**: Ferretti was responsible for every aspect of the design. He reconstructed Tibet in Morocco; he used CGI to recreate the Himalayan back-drop; he designed 1,800 costumes and bought all the fabrics in India: "The job couldn't be split between production and costume designers as normal; I felt the film should resemble a tapestry, so every aspect of the design had to be integrated." (1) Terrace Potala Palace. (2) Peking Square. (3) Dungkar terrace. (5) The family kitchen. (6) Exterior of Potala. (7) Throne room, Potala Palace. (8) Scene in the throne room. (9–10) Potala Palace details.

(1–7) **Interview with the Vampire**: Ferretti created an integrated look by contrasting visually the scenes set in New Orleans (using intense colours to evoke the stifling atmosphere of the swamp) and Paris (using darker, more muted colours). (2) The swamp. (3–4) Apartment interiors. (5) Vampire Theatre and (6–7) catacombs (the design of which was influenced by the painter Piranesi).

attacked by the Turks. When we realised we didn't have the money to build it in Cinecittà, I remembered a location in Spain I had scouted for another project years earlier – Belchite, a town which had been bombed in the Spanish Civil War, and never rebuilt. It was like a ghost town, perfect for the scene.

Pasolini liked to work on location because it gave the film a sense of reality. Fellini only used locations as a source of inspiration. For example, once we drove out of Rome to go to the seaside. We spent hours staring at the sea, studying it, trying to figure out how we could recreate it in the studio! Then, on the way back home, he suddenly stopped the car as we passed some fields where tomatoes were being cultivated. The crop was all under plastic which caught the light as it moved in the wind. Fellini exclaimed, "It looks like the sea..." That was how we created the sea in **And the Ship Sails On**. With Fellini, everything was built in the studio – and for me, that is real production design. An empty stage is to a production designer what the blank page is to a writer. **And the Ship Sails On** was the ultimate challenge: creating an ocean liner at sea in the studio.

And the Ship Sails On is my favourite film, but **Kundun** is the most extraordinary film I've worked on. We had hoped to shoot the film in India, but the Indian government, under pressure from China, refused to give us permission. Instead, we decided to base the film in Morocco (where I had worked with Pasolini). I recreated the Lhasa exteriors in the Atlas Mountains, and built an entire soundstage in a warehouse for the interiors of the Potala Palace (which I was able to recreate thanks to a floor plan that the Dalai Lama sketched for me). Everything was built for the film; thanks to CGI, I was even able to alter the landscape so that it looked more Tibetan. For the first time, I also designed the costumes for the film. I felt obliged to do this because they were integral to the overall design of the film, which I wanted to look like a tapestry. My efforts were rewarded when the Tibetan actors arrived in Morocco and saw the sets. They began to cry, and thanked me for giving them back their country. Subsequently, I was approached by a delegation of Tibetans including several relatives of the Dalai Lama who asked me, in the event that they ever are able to reclaim Tibet, to come to help them rebuild it. I've done many films which are important to me, but this experience was the most special.

The collaboration of Dean Tavoularis with Francis Ford Coppola has yielded some of the most striking design in contemporary cinema: the stunning depiction of New York from the turn of the century to the present day in **The Godfather** trilogy (1972–1990); the glorious theatricality and studio spectacle of **One from the Heart** (1982); the meticulously detailed naturalism of **The Conversation**

dean tavoularis

63

interview

(1974); the stylised monochrome urban vistas of **Rumble Fish** (1983); the nightmarish evocation of the insanity and horror of war in **Apocalypse Now** (1979). For Coppola, Tavoularis also designed **The Outsiders** (1983), **Peggy Sue Got Married** (1986), **Tucker: The Man and His Dream** (1988) and **Jack** (1996), as well as Coppola productions such as **The Escape Artist** (1982, Caleb Deschanel) and **Hammett** (1983, Wim Wenders). He designed **Zabriskie Point** (1970) for Antonioni, and **The Ninth Gate** (1999) for Polanski. He has also worked twice with Arthur Penn, on **Bonnie and Clyde** (1967) and **Little Big Man** (1970). It is a filmography characterised by an extraordinary diversity of design styles; but whatever the subject, Tavoularis' eye for telling detail unfailingly draws you deep into the world he creates for the camera.

When I was a student, I didn't know anything about film-making. It wasn't until I was working at Disney as an animator that I began to learn of the existence of the art department, but as it happened, my college background was ideal for a career in production design. I studied architecture and fine art. The former taught me how to think in terms of the volume of a space; the latter taught me how to use colour. Volume and colour are my key raw materials when I'm thinking about how to create a sense of atmosphere in a film. From the architectural point of view, I like to layer space to give a sense of depth; there's always something going on further back – a view into another room, or through a window. With colour, I like to create layers of contrast in a set using different colours from foreground to background.

My first reading of a script is always very important. I like to read it very quickly in one sitting. Right away, I'll start to get impressions and images that help me to visualise the film. But

1

2

(1–8) **Apocalypse Now**: Tavoularis read Conrad's 'Heart of Darkness' and the Bible when researching. "Like Conrad, the story is a journey into the soul of man, which gets darker and more complex as it develops." (1–2) Low- and high-angle production illustrations. (4–7) Storyboard.

3

① CONT. CAM. MOVING THROUGH JUNGLE QUICKLY WITH ONE VIETNAMESE — BREATHLESSLY RUNNING FOR HIS LIFE — LEAVES, BARK, ETC. FLYING

QUICK CUT - CLOSE RUNNING - TO CAM -

4

① CONT —

AMERICAN BENDS TO CAM - EXTREME CLOSE-UP.
- WEARING JUNGLE HAT - PEACE SIGN -
REACHES TO US W/LG KNIFE -
PREPARING TO SCALP THE DEAD -
IN BACKGROUND - HUT, WHITE, BURNING —
FIGURE BECOMES VERY SOFT - DARK.

TO - RUNNING SANDALS OF
VIETNAMESE SOLDIER,
MOVING FASTER & FASTER -
MOVES WITH IN
SUDDENLY HE STOPS —

5

6

LA CUT - PAINTED
AMERICAN W/SPEAR -
SPEAR FILLS SCREEN

EXPLOSION

8

65

dean tavoularis

EX CU - OUR VIEW FALLS WITHIN
TO THE GROUND - EXPLODING AND
SCATTER ABOVE US —

7

SUDDEN CUT —
ANOTHER SAVAGE LOOKING
AMERICAN — OPENS HIS
FLAME-THROWER DIRECTLY ON US —

COMPLETELY FILLS
THE SCREEN WITH ME.

(1–3) **One From the Heart**: Tavoularis created an opulent, extravagant vision of Las Vegas on the lot of Zoetrope Studios. (4–6) **The Godfather** trilogy: Over a 10-hour meeting, Tavoularis, director Coppola and D.P. Gordon Willis evolved the classical tableau style of the films. Tavoularis created meticulously detailed and layered sets to add visual depth, as well as consistency to the many periods and locations seen in the three films. The repeated use of oranges – here glimpsed behind Sofia Coppola (6) – as props was not intended as a symbol, as claimed by some critics. Tavoularis simply felt the fruit added colour and showed up well in Willis' photography.

more importantly, I like to get an idea of what the story is really about in the simplest terms – is it a quest for something or someone, or a story about two people getting together? **Bonnie and Clyde** seemed to me to be about two renegades rebelling against the world they lived in. **Apocalypse Now** was about the infernal madness of war. **The Godfather**, which Paramount viewed as just another gangster picture, was about a family and the American dream. Once I've established the thrust of the story for myself, I keep referring back to it in everything I do. Subsequent discussions with the director will obviously help to illuminate or sharpen your process; it's their movie, after all, not the designer's.

I get a lot from hanging out socially with directors I work with. I don't like to question them too directly about the film, I prefer to talk more generally. It's important to get a good, clear idea of who they are in order to understand what kind of film they want to make – and they are all different. I love working with Francis Coppola, because we've known each other for years. We always talk about future projects he hopes to make which I like because a designer typically only goes to work on a film when he's hired, ten to 20 weeks before shooting begins. My relationship with Coppola means I start thinking about the film sometimes years before it is even financed.

It is not always easy to gain a director's trust. When I first met Michelangelo Antonioni to discuss **Zabriskie Point**, I was in awe of him. Seeing **L'Avventura** and **Red Desert** had been seminal film-going experiences for me when I was a student (I was always more inspired by European cinema than what

was coming out of Hollywood). But Antonioni was not easy to collaborate with initially; introverted, and very suspicious whenever I tried to tell him what my intentions were. His response to any idea was always on the lines of "No, no, no, no". After three weeks of preparation, he was due to fly back to Rome, but he still seemed to be very uncomfortable about what I was giving him. So after his departure, I went back to my office at MGM and made sketches based on everything we had talked about. I had photographs taken of all the furniture that I was proposing to use. I made a presentation just as an interior designer does with a client: fabric swatches, colour charts, perspective drawings from different angles which we glued on to beautiful boards. Then I made a huge box with individual slots for all these elements and sent it to him in Rome. Michelangelo being a very particular person, it was very important that what I sent him wasn't some dingy little sketch in a crumpled envelope with a note saying, "how about this?" Well, he received the package and when he returned to the U.S. he was a different person. At last, he felt secure with me.

Production design requires both sides of the brain. Only about 10–20% of the job is about having ideas and designing. It doesn't matter how talented you are in creative terms, if you're not well-organised and logical about how you approach the job, or you're unable to manage people or work to budgets and deadlines, it will kill you. When I begin working on a film, almost the first thing I do is set up my office where I can sit down to work and make phone calls. At this point of the process, you're making several kinds of decisions apart from the actual design ones. You're listing everything that needs to be researched. You're finding locations. You're hiring your crew. It's essential to surround yourself with a strong team: a good art director and construction manager will take some of the responsibility off your shoulders so you don't have to spend every waking minute worrying about the money and the time you have.

My own work process depends on research. I love research, sometimes to the point where I'm in danger of forgetting the movie. But it's the way I penetrate the world of the film. I read novels or history books related to the material. I accumulate picture material to trigger ideas. In a period film, every detail is vital. Every piece of dressing has to be appropriate, although you should avoid cluttering a set with all the iconic objects of the period. You have to find the ordinary, everyday things – which is difficult because there aren't so many pictures of them. Research is also about going to flea markets or shops with the set decorator to find bric-a-brac. Whether it's a period or a contemporary story, one should always think about what possessions a character might have in their environment. Gene Hackman's apartment in **The Conversation** was deliberately bare, as is Johnny Depp's in **The Ninth Gate**. Both their characters are focused to an obsessive degree on their work. Neither have families, nor hobbies. Hackman, a surveillance spy, simply had a work area where he could tinker with his devices; Depp, an antique book dealer, was surrounded by books. In both cases, the tools of their respective trades made for visually interesting set dressing.

When I began to research the teepees required for **Little Big Man**, I was told, "Everyone has teepees. All the studios have made films with Indians." I went down to Fox to look at some. They were grotesque, orange with yellow zig-zags, made from suede, with stitching an inch apart. So we started to do our own research, and discovered a Cheyenne tepee in a museum in Pasadena. It was a revelation. It was stitched as if by a surgeon, meticulously, to make it properly waterproof. It was made from buffalo skin, very thin and translucent so when you put a light in it at night, it glowed. We decided to manufacture our own teepees. I found a tannery in downtown L.A. We purchased the cow hides, sewed them together as invisibly as we could, then put them through a machine that shaved the whole skin down. We tinted them a muddy, cream colour, then cut them to the right dimensions. After that, there was no going back. Everything had to match the same standard of authenticity we'd set ourselves: arrows, spears, harnesses, the beadwork, the racks for beef jerky. We replicated the Indians' traditional materials, which of course came from nature. The colour pigments they used in their war paint, for example, gave us a very earthy, organic colour palette for the film – bright yellows or ultramarine blues weren't available. We vetoed anything that was wrong, which antagonised a lot of people. "How dare you, we've been doing Indian pictures for years..." was a common refrain. I'd reply, "Yes, but all the Indian pictures are wrong. Let's try to make this one a little better." We were rewarded after a screening in New York attended by some people from 'American Heritage' magazine; they thanked us for being the first film-makers to show respect for the way the Indians lived.

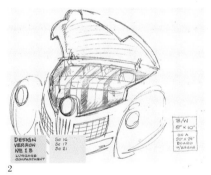

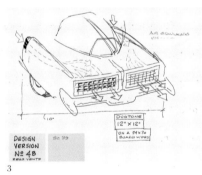

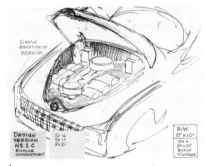

2
3
4

(2–4) Tavoularis' sketches based on the
visionary automobile design by the hero of
Coppola's biographical film, **Tucker** (1–4).

SCENE 106

...PORTHOLE

MOVE INTO PORTHOLE

MATCH CUT....

1

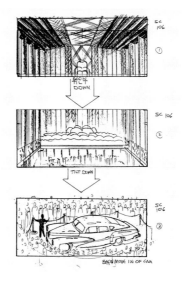

BEGIN TILT DOWN

TILT DOWN

BEGIN MOVE IN ON CAR

2

"SUPERTITLES MENTION WHEREVER TUCKER IS"

3

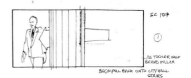

TUCKER LEAVES THE PARAMOUNT NIGHT FADES TO BLACK

AS TUCKER HALF BEHIND PILLAR

BEGIN PULL BACK ONTO CITY HALL STAIRS

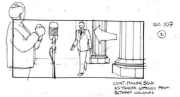

CONT. PULLING BACK AS TUCKER APPEARS FROM BETWEEN COLUMNS

4

PARAMOUNT THEATRE (SHADED)   CITY HALL STEPS (SHADED)

NOTE:
• MATCH RATE OF PAN
• MATCH LIGHT ON COLUMN

5

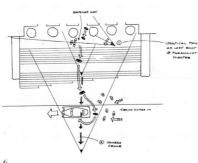

6

(1–5) **Tucker**: storyboard for the sequence shot in two different locations (Paramount Theatre and City Hall steps). The columns are used to create a seamless transition (4–5).

7

Conventional practice on a movie is that you build some things in the studio and you find other things as locations. My personal preference is to build on location. Any location you find can become a set, because by the time you've finished with it, you might have changed it by 50%. When we began working on **The Godfather**, Paramount wanted us to shoot it all on their permanent New York set, which is nothing like New York. Francis and I had to battle to try to bring the film to New York. I've always loved the New York film style pioneered by Kazan with his cameraman Boris Kaufman shooting in real bars or pool hills – it has real grit. We wanted this kind of reality for **The Godfather** films. **The Godfather Part II** required a huge street set for the scenes depicting Vito Corleone's early life. I drove around New York with the location guy looking for something that resembled the reference photograph of Little Italy in 1912 which I had taped to the windscreen of our car. At last, we found a street in the Ukrainian district which we thought might work. We started knocking on doors and chatting to people who – fortunately for us – were very interested in the history of the area and showed us a basement museum devoted to the first Ukrainian immigrants who arrived around the same time as the Italians in our story. To use the street in the film, we had to approach everyone who lived there, some 300 people. We changed everything – the lights, the signage; we had to close down several businesses (including the funeral parlour); we built new stores, put gravel on the roads. It took six months of construction work in total.

Building on location can be like Fitzcarraldo hauling his steamship over the mountain. On **Apocalypse Now**, it was important for the story that the temple set for the climax should be located in really dense, wild jungle – this was the destination the whole film had been heading towards, its heart of darkness. Finding the location was hard enough; but then getting the 600 people it took to build it there, and transporting supplies and food becomes a major undertaking. Everything had to be brought in on bamboo sleds pulled by caribou – there was no way a truck could have got there. We started to build it when production started (we were shooting in continuity) so it was ready by the end of the shoot. We used traditional Philippine building methods, which were similar to those of the Montagnard tribe of Vietnam. There were no power tools; everything was built manually using machetes to cut the bamboo and palm fronds.

I used a lot of red coloration in the temple set to suggest insanity, and also death, just as in **The Godfather Part II**, we tried to impregnate the film with intimations of mortality by using purples, browns, blacks (the use of oranges in the trilogy, however, had no symbolic value as has been supposed; it was just a good contrast to the darker tones we used). Right now, I'm interested in further exploring the possibilities of colour in film design. On **Bulworth**, I took a long strip of paper and noted down each important beat in the story continuity. Underneath it, I created a band with a spectrum of colours to reflect the dramatic development of the story, starting from an absence of colour at the beginning of the film. I always relish the opportunity to do something new on a film.

biography

Growing up in Norwich, Stuart Craig knew he didn't want a career in insurance or banking. He gravitated to art school and theatre design. At the Royal College of Art, he designed student film projects before a job as art department runner on **Casino Royale** ("a spectacularly dreadful film") launched him on a 12-year apprenticeship in the art department. **The Elephant Man** (1980, David Lynch) established him

stuart craig

internationally as a production designer; he is now one of the most sought-after designers working today, a winner of three Oscars. Responsible for epic designs on **Gandhi** (1982, Richard Attenborough), **Greystoke** (1984, Hugh Hudson), **The Mission** (1986, Roland Joffé) and **The English Patient** (1996, Anthony Minghella) – he also created the more intimate settings of **Dangerous Liaisons** (1988, Stephen Frears), **The Secret Garden** (1993, Agnieszka Holland) and **Shadowlands** (1993, Richard Attenborough). It is with some sadness that Craig looks back on the failures of two recent films which represented a huge design effort – **Mary Reilly** (1996, Stephen Frears) and **The Avengers** (1998, Jeremiah Chechik). Meanwhile, he has defied his industry typecasting for period films by designing the contemporary comedy **Notting Hill** (1999, Roger Michell).

interview

Production design is not simply a question of designing the images – one also has to design the way the money and effort is expended. The designer addresses the script and the amount of money available and offers the producer a viable way of making the film. I might suggest, for example, that what is in the script can't be found in the real world – or needs to be treated theatrically – and therefore the film should be shot in the studio. Or, that it would be better to shoot in one country rather than another – for practical or aesthetic reasons. These decisions affect not just the look of the film, but the entire production process. There are two divisions within the art department. The first is focused on the drawing-board, where the sets are designed and blueprints produced: technical plans drawn to scale which are then relayed to the construction crew, the carpenters, plasterers and painters. The second division is for the set dressing, furnishings and props. The production designer straddles the two areas. My own apprenticeship was served on the

'THE ELEPHANT MAN' INTo ISOLATION WARD - LONDON HOSPITAL

2

(1–3) **The Elephant Man**: (1) Pencil sketch for the interior of the isolation ward: "I like the definite placement of these very simple objects, the enigmatic quality of the shrouded elephant man, and the little window on the floor." (2–3) "When the elephant man is exhibited as a freak in a Belgian circus, his master tells a preposterous tale about how his mother was raped by an elephant on a desert island. The drawing for the circus poster was an illustration of the showman's patter." (4–5) **Dangerous Liaisons**: Financial limitations meant that most of the film was shot in close up: in design terms, this meant an emphasis on texture rather than large three-dimensional sets. "It was about how the fabric of a costume played against the upholstery, or the furniture against a wall."

architectural side, so my basic working tools are the drawing and the model. I served a 12-year apprenticeship, working my way up from junior draftsman to art director. It was a very old-fashioned training; these days, the expectation of film school graduates is that they will begin to work in their chosen specialisation sooner – but this is at odds with the surprisingly conservative nature of the film business. Producers always want new talent but the financial stages are high. New talent gets hired easily the second time, but, unproven, it struggles desperately for the first break. The options are to work in short films, pop videos, commercials and then break into features; or to suspend one's ambitions and do a long apprenticeship. Certainly, I would encourage every young designer to surround themselves with people who are more experienced or more able; it gives you something to draw on.

I'm sure that you could take a snatch of conversation in Richard Rogers' office, or Tricia Guild's, or an art department's – and it would be impossible to identify which it came from. We all talk in the same kind of language. However, it's very important to understand that the design of a film has nothing to do with interior design or fashion. We are serving a dramatic art; taste in film design is about making choices which are appropriate for the story. It's for this reason that I never choose to work on a project on the basis of the design opportunities it offers – what interests me is the script or the director. It doesn't matter what kind of film it is – period, science fiction, thriller or comedy – the discipline remains the same. There's always the opportunity to design

something well. **Shadowlands** remains one of my best-achieved films in design terms; although extremely simple and modest in ambition by comparison to others I have designed, I feel we made some good design choices. The scale of C.S. Lewis' house in the film – influenced by the Arts and Crafts style and the great architect Voysey – was very simple but struck just the right note of sophistication. It was also very English.

John Barry, the brilliant designer of such films as **A Clockwork Orange** and **Star Wars** who died tragically young, used to say that the best sets are based on one key idea. And it's really true. Ultimately, the best film design is incredibly simple. My whole process is aimed at achieving simplicity. I always start with doodles, full of confusion, devoid of focus. Thereafter it's a process of elimination. As I sift through all the clutter, I begin to accept certain ideas and reject others, and in so doing an attitude is formed. One of the key tools in this process of elimination is polarisation. I always look for contrast in the drama, because it really helps to shape and define the visual approach. Something is only big when it's placed alongside something that is small. In **The Secret Garden**, the contrast is between the cold, forbidding mansion and the magical garden. In **The English Patient** it's between pre-war North Africa and post-war Italy; the opulence of Cairo and the austerity of the Tuscan monastery. In **Mary Reilly**, it's between Mary's sensitivity and fragility, and her brutal environment in which everything seems designed to intimidate her.

1

2

3

4

5

6

7

8

11

(1–12) **The Secret Garden**: (1) Mary at the feet of the Buddha in India: "we made the figure of the Buddha in perspective except the feet which were full size." (2–4) Everything in the Yorkshire mansion was designed to dwarf the figure of Mary and make her vulnerable whereas the secret garden (5–8) represented a magical haven. Craig read books about horticulturist Gertrude Jekyll and visited Sissinghurst for inspiration. (9) Fabric swatches for bed and curtains in (10, 12) Colin's room.

stuart craig

INT. JEKYLL'S BEDROOM

3

1

4

2

EXT. COURTYARD
JEKYLL'S HOUSE

5

6

7

11

8

12

"MARY REILLY" EXT SIDE STREET

9

"MARY REILLY" EXT RED LIGHT DISTRICT

10

(1–12) **Mary Reilly**: Director Stephen Frears suggested the Jekyll and Hyde story could be relocated to Edinburgh. "The city had an altogether more dramatic quality of the 19th century than London, with its stone blackened by industrial pollution, and the way it sits either side of a big canyon with the castle mound rising out of it." Craig's design sought to echo and exaggerate Edinburgh's architectural landscape while interiors such as Jekyll's bedroom (3) and library (1, 4) had a classical, monumental quality. "Everything in the film was designed to be intimidating to Mary."

The art department has to make an infinite number of choices on a film, big and small, but all significant. While I might be deciding what country the film would best be shot in, Stephenie McMillan, my set decorator, might be choosing which tablecloth or napkins or ashtrays belong in the set. Polarisation helps you to eliminate the middle ground, the grey areas. It helps you to discern between what is necessary and extraneous, right and wrong, good and bad, appropriate and inappropriate. Gradually, it becomes obvious what belongs – and you might begin to reject some idea or location you loved in the first week of preparation, because it no longer fits into the jigsaw. On **Gandhi**, the art director taught me a trick I've never forgotten. After we returned from a recce in India, he stuck all the snapshots we'd taken of the locations on the walls of our office in script order. It was an excellent idea, not only because it helped us to get an overview of a logistically very complex project, but because it gave us an immediate read-out of how the film progressed visually, with all its contrasts and juxtapositions. I've continued to apply this method ever since, adding my design sketches.

The process of elimination is obviously helped by research. On **The English Patient**, I found myself in the archive of the Royal Geographical Society opening the same files and looking at the same documents and photographs of the real Count Almasy as both novelist Michael Ondaatje and writer/director Anthony Minghella had done before me. It gave me a precious insight into how this source material had become fiction. Following in the writer's footsteps and seeing what they have chosen to exploit or reject in turn helps me to

decide what is relevant. But the director's choices must be paramount. **Dangerous Liaisons** was relatively low-budget for a period film with American stars. The producers pressurised director Stephen Frears and me to scout locations in Hungary. They'd heard that labour and facilities were cheap there. (Considerations such as whether Budapest could stand in architecturally for 18th-century France weren't relevant; in the Hollywood mind-set, it's old, it's European, so what's the problem?) Everything we saw on the recce reinforced my resistance to the idea. Digging the heels in, we convinced them to recce around Paris instead. Of course, we immediately found everything we were looking for – but the added expense meant we would not be able to go beyond the immediate city environs (there was no money for hotel accommodation); neither would we be able to feature spectacular wide shots filled with carriages, nor fill a chateau with beautiful dressing. Stephen was smart enough to turn these limitations into a virtue. He realised that the story was about the thought processes and mind-games of the characters, the sexual tensions and political intrigues – and he decided to approach the film as a series of close-ups. This immediately reduced the financial pressures; instead of showing a whole room, we focused on a corner, featuring maybe a door, the bed and two walls. Set design is mostly sculptural – three-dimensional; in this case it became textural. The focus was on how the texture of a costume fabric played against a piece of upholstery, for example.

On **Notting Hill**, the reality of the film's setting is characterised by teeming confusion. We could have said,

(1–3) **The English Patient**: (1) Almasy's Cairo bedroom, seen in the film's flashback narrative. Its exotic opulence was a counterpoint to the austere simplicity of the room in the Tuscan monastery in which he remembers his past as he lies dying from burn injuries. (2) Photocopy given by director Anthony Minghella to set decorator Stephenie MacMillan, a reference for the Cairo bazaar set. (3) MacMillan's own research snapshot. Craig: "I leave a great deal to Stephenie and I trust her implicitly. While I'm working out the big design problems of the movie, it's a relief to know that someone else is being equally attentive to the details."

1

7

5

6

production design & art direction

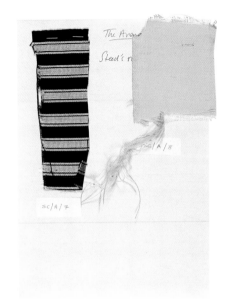

3

8

4

(1–8) **The Avengers**: Craig's epic, almost abstract drawings for the film were influenced by the stylisation of the original television series. When designing Steed's town house, Craig's aim was to extend the character's flashy style beyond his bowler hat and Bentley. "A visit to the John Soane Museum gave me the key: the Georgian drawing room walls were lined with brilliant chrome yellow silk. It seemed the perfect statement for the character." (5) The location found for Steed's home, before and (6) after the art department moved in. (2) Fabric swatches picked out by Stephenie MacMillan for the silk-lined wall and soft furnishings.

that's the reality, let's go and shoot it on the streets. Ultimately, however, we decided to recreate it in the studio; not because we wanted to idealise it, but because it gave us complete control over how we presented the confusion. Everything was there because we had chosen it and physically placed it there. We also had control over the "weather" and the light. I think it's always preferable to build in the studio if you can. All location shooting is full of the potential need to compromise (it's not quite what you wanted, the relationship to the sun isn't as you'd have liked, etc.). You're always somehow struggling against the world. **Gandhi** was a tremendous effort of which I was proud to be a part, but the chaotic reality of shooting in contemporary India forced so many compromises on us; the design was not always under control. Film-making is like a production line; all the different elements are so compartmentalised. The writer produces a screenplay, then the designer begins to visualise it, then the cinematographer comes in, then the actors, then the editor goes to work on the rushes, then the composer writes the music... Despite the presence of a director overseeing the process, one is always fighting against the separate nature of these functions. Ralph Fiennes was incredibly interested and involved with the sets for **The English Patient**; he clearly fed off our work, and because producer Saul Zaentz is generous in the way he schedules his films, he was around early enough for us to be able to feed off his ideas. Such opportunities are all too rare, but it is absolutely essential for a film's design and cinematography to coincide. When I design, I think primarily in terms of composition – where the actor is going to be in relation to the camera and the light source. I care more about the composition of a shot than a detail of panelling. There's a degree of trepidation in how one first approaches the D.P., because to some degree the designer has already lit the set by deciding where the windows will be, or where the practical lights are. I try to see the D.P. as early as possible and show him the models and drawings, and ask him about his preferences. When his ideas build from this then the process is working well. I like to be on the set before shooting begins in order to explain a shot I had in mind when the set was conceived; once the camera set-up is finalised, I rearrange the dressing accordingly. It's like a series of chess moves. You learn how things look on film; for example, skin tones are predominately red-based, so greens or greys are the most sympathetic and complimentary background. I love working with brave cinematographers like Philippe Rousselot, who used a really soft light with no contrast whatsoever on **Mary Reilly** – yielding a slight glow in the endless murk. Some in the art department were terribly upset because you could scarcely see the lovingly-crafted detail in the sets; but I thought it was phenomenal and wholly original. You have to be able to let go of your work and hand it on.

The digital revolution has made so much more possible in design terms. Undoubtedly, in the future, more and more elements of a film will be computer-generated. The designer will have to be able to add the computer to his working-tools, but also the schedule will have to be amended, either so that more effects shots are created during shooting, or so that the designer continues working on the film into post-production.

Before becoming a production designer, von Brandenstein worked as set decorator, costume designer (**Saturday Night Fever**, 1977, John Badham), scenic artist (**Hair**, 1979, Milos Forman) and art director (**Ragtime**, 1981, Milos Forman). She established herself as a designer on films such as the coming-of-age story **Breaking Away** (1979, Peter Yates) and the frontier drama **Heartland** (1979, Richard Pearce, for

patrizia von brandenstein

whom she also designed **Leap of Faith**, 1992) and has since worked in a variety of genres and period settings: the musical (**A Chorus Line**, 1985, Richard Attenborough); screwball comedy (**The Money Pit**, 1985, Richard Benjamin); thriller (**Mercury Rising**, 1998, Harold Becker; **A Simple Plan**, 1999, Sam Raimi, for whom she also designed the western **The Quick and the Dead**, 1995); gangster movie (**The Untouchables**, 1987, Brian De Palma); social comedy (**Six Degrees of Separation**, 1993, Fred Schepisi); political drama (**Silkwood**, 1983, Mike Nichols, for whom she also designed **Working Girl**, 1988 and **Postcards from the Edge**, 1990). For Milos Forman, she designed **Amadeus** (1984, for which she received an Oscar), **The People vs. Larry Flynt** (1996) and **Man on the Moon** (1999).

interview

I was 30 years old before I set foot on a movie set. Theatre was my training ground and my first love. As the daughter of an army officer – an "army brat" – I grew up in Paris and, aged 14, I enrolled in a youth programme at the Comédie Française. Students were rotated around the different backstage departments, so I was able to learn about all the traditional theatre crafts – scene-painting, wig-making, wardrobe, prop-making. When I later settled in New York, I put this invaluable education to good use. I had the good fortune to fall in with the Actors' Studio, which was at the time expanding and beginning to put on its own productions. This background (as well as my peripatetic upbringing which exposed me to a variety of foreign cultures in Europe and Mexico) meant that by the time I began working on movies, I had a very thorough, solid technical and aesthetic foundation for a career in production design. The day I first went on to a movie set, I thought; "this is what I want to do for the rest of my life". My break came when a set decorator suddenly quit

1

5

production design & art direction

2

6

3

4

7

8

9

10

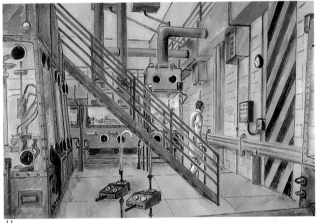

11

(1–8) **Ragtime**: "I build on location all the time: that's my trademark." (2) The Lower East Side street set, created on East 11th Street in Manhattan. (3–4) Period photos used to research the set. (5–8) Sketches for street characters: "I often do studies like this on period films as an aid to set dressing and props." (9–11) **Silkwood**: Unable to access ground plans of a nuclear plant (such visual material being classified information), von Brandenstein sought out a retired plant engineer who talked her through the layout of the interior, enabling her to design the set. The leeched coloration of the plant was in contrast to the warm colours used elsewhere in the film to evoke the lyricism and simplicity of rural life in Oklahoma.

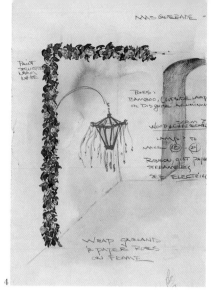

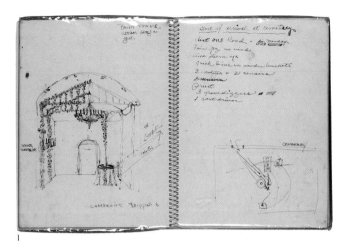

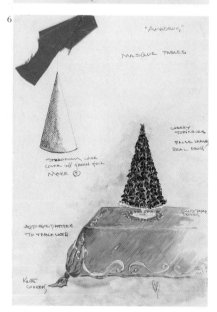

(1–7) **Amadeus**: (1) Pages from von Brandenstein's workbook show the plan for the cemetery for Mozart's burial and a rough sketch for the masquerade scene which was shot on location at Kromeriz Castle in Prague. (2) Production sketch for the masquerade: "We were prohibited from putting up lights or decor. The major design problem was to light from chandeliers with no apparent fixings. We hung chandeliers (with practical candles) off the frame of the gazebo, which was built to be free-standing and decorated to mask the electrics." (4–7) "Sketches of the lanterns, draperies, food topiaries and mask-seller – done to brief the set dressers as our time in the masquerade location was limited and the work extensive."

on Michael Ritchie's film, **The Candidate**. I just happened to be in the right place at the right time and was interviewed by the designer who asked me, "Can you start now?" "Sure," I replied. So he told me to get in the car and go off and find a hospital E.R. to shoot in. "Oh," I said, "and when do we need it for?" "In a couple of hours..." I drove wildly off down the freeway, ran into the first hospital I could find and threw myself at the administrator: "You've GOT to help me! This is my big chance!" To my astonishment and delight, he agreed; 90 minutes later, the cast and crew rolled up.

I guess everyone who works in film is infected with a Pygmalion complex: we all want to breathe life into the script. The job of a production designer is to translate the screenplay visually. A film is like a mosaic, and each piece has to relate to the whole. I think in terms of what a scene is trying to say, more than trying to be the characters' interior decorator. I am not interested in decor *per se*; the most beautiful ballroom on earth means nothing unless it helps the context of the story. My design process is pretty much the same whether the film is epic or intimate, whatever it's genre or period. When I begin working on a film, I feel like I'm casting a great net out to sea and gathering in everything that gets caught within it. I'll sift through my catch until I find the image that to me distils what the film is about. The image evolves through the process of talking with the director, doing the research, choosing the locations. I know I've found it when it begins to crop up everywhere I look – repeating itself in the pattern of the pipes or the layout of a floor... It's sort of like being paranoid. Because I'm a colourist at heart, the colours in the

image are key; but so too is the sense of its mass and shape, and how these things reflect the nature of the story.

On **Saturday Night Fever**, for example, the image of John Travolta's white suit had an iconic significance within the story. We wanted to make a world where people came alive on Saturday night, lived for Saturday night, expressed their true selves on Saturday night (the rest of the week was putting in time). For **Working Girl**, the image in my mind was the huddled masses approaching Manhattan on the Staten Island ferry; to Melanie Griffiths, this city is like a marvellous Oz that she yearns to enter (despite the fact that it's a world populated by despicable people – an irony Mike Nichols picked up on brilliantly). Sometimes the image forms with the help of a reference. While working on **Postcards from the Edge**, I had a reproduction of one of Hockney's Polaroid collages pinned to my wall; to me it expressed the fragmented nature of Meryl Streep's existence, her confusion over what was and wasn't real. Jim Carrey in **Man on the Moon** suffers from a similar affliction as he juggles three levels of reality: the overblown hyper-reality of the television studio, the real world beyond it and his fantasy life. The image I kept coming back to was the solitary performer isolated in the darkness by a bright spotlight. I thought of Al Capone in **The Untouchables** as a gangland Sun King; the world revolves around him. That's where the central motif on the floor in the opening shot came from, with rays radiating out from him.

Like Capone, I felt that Larry and Althea in **The People vs. Larry Flynt** were mythical characters: like the protagonists

production design & art direction

1

2

3

4

5

6

(1–3): **Just Cause**: "We built the prison set which held the deranged prisoner's cell (1) in 17 days, an incredibly short time. Then we created the jungle set (2–3) in a Miami warehouse (six months later, it had to be rebuilt for reshoots in London to accommodate Sean Connery's schedule)." (4–6) **The Untouchables**: A magazine ad for a brooch was the inspiration for the floor motif (4) which defined Al Capone as a "gangland Sun King" in the opening scene. (5) Illustration for the courtroom set. (6) Pencil rough of the exterior of the elevated railway, scene of the first bomb explosion. "The tavern speakeasy which got blown up was in reality a Chicago sushi bar!"

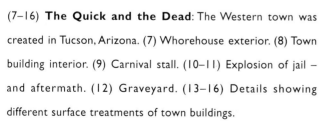

(7–16) **The Quick and the Dead**: The Western town was created in Tucson, Arizona. (7) Whorehouse exterior. (8) Town building interior. (9) Carnival stall. (10–11) Explosion of jail – and aftermath. (12) Graveyard. (13–16) Details showing different surface treatments of town buildings.

in a Greek tragedy. The sexually-charged, turgid quality to their lives and his obsessive self-aggrandisement seemed to me to demand the colour purple. Colour was also essential to the organising principle behind **Amadeus**, where I was profoundly influenced by the music. Mozart's music seemed fresh and modern to me; it was expressive of the Age of Enlightenment, it was bright and reflective, like a mirror, or floating light. It implied a colour spectrum from silver to pale pastels – rose, blue, yellow, green – and fabrics like satin or silk. Salieri's music, by contrast, seemed to come from an earlier era. It had a heavier quality, solid, stolid. It implied darker colours, ochre, heavy gold, dark reds and greens. It seemed to call for velvet. Once this contrast became clear to me, I wanted it to be reflected in every aspect of the decor.

Sometimes the research process is very specific – what did school buses in 1979 New York look like? I'll usually delegate this to an assistant, who will look it up on the Internet and try to get a picture reference. Other times, it requires the designer to be like an investigative journalist. How do you design the interior of a nuclear power station (for **Silkwood**) when all the related visual material is classified information? I was fortunate to find a retired engineer who had left government service. Naturally, he didn't have any pictures, so I had to question him about every detail. As he talked, I drew. I'd ask, "what does a rod look like? Is it two-inches wide? Or one inch? How long? If you draw a section, how thick is it...?" He talked me through the process of the slurry and the slugging press and the reverse-flow air system used to catch the particles. Gradually I was able to

create a picture of it. A lot of the machinery was made in the art department out of cardboard, and our decorator found a kind of scrap heap of nuclear plant equipment in New Mexico where we obtained stuff like gauges, valves and levers which we adapted for the set. Even though I made the interior a little bigger than reality, we had observers come down during the shoot who thought it was a pretty authentic set.

Sometimes the research involves having to immerse yourself in an unfamiliar world in order then to be able to translate it to the requirements of the story. So for **Leap of Faith**, I needed to learn about faith healers and psychics and crystals. And for **Amadeus**, it was essential to learn about the structure of the court (paramount to our story) and understand the background to the script. I went through Mozart's tax rolls, which revealed that he actually made quite a bit of money from his music (it was sold in the market-place). Yet he died in poverty. We became convinced that he was a gambler. He was in a very fast crowd and there are hints in his letters that he had gambling debts. I learned how he spent his money, his love of fine clothes, and how terribly his wife managed their affairs. They were a reckless, feckless theatrical couple. And I discovered that he moved house ten times; although in a film it would be confusing for an audience if we showed him in ten different places. My research enabled me to use the one apartment we did show in order to convey his rootlessness. The apartment gradually empties through the film (as his finances deteriorate and he loses his possessions to the pawnbrokers of Vienna). Milos Forman's attitude to authenticity on **Amadeus** was summed up in a sentence: "tell

patrizia von brandenstein

(1–7) **The People vs. Larry Flynt**: "After I read the script and researched the background, I thought, this is like a Greek tragedy. Flynt was an extreme character, an egocentric who invented and mythologised himself – I wanted to reflect that scenically." (1) Flynt's childhood home. (2) First Hustler club in Cleveland ("I like to paint on unconventional surfaces – mirrors, glass or linoleum"). (3) Flynt's first office. (4) Flynt's mansion. (5) The Supreme Court set. (6) "The sexually-charged, turgid quality to the Flynt's lives and Larry Flynt's obsessive self-aggrandisement seemed to me to demand the colour purple."

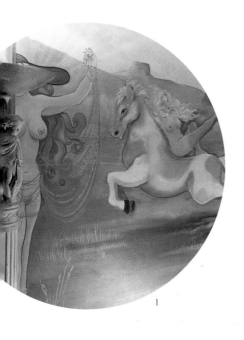

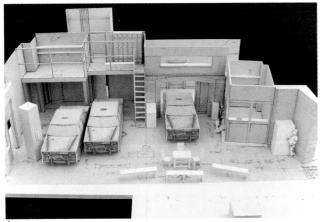

(1–7) **Man on the Moon**: (2) Carnegie Hall model and (3) completed set. (4) Model for *Taxi* set and (5) completed set: "For years I depended on sketches and photos to convey set information to the director, but now I have a new weapon in the arsenal which I love to use: tiny, compact video cameras bring fluidity and motion to my set models as well as the nascent sense of drama inherent in any camera." (6) Lake Tahoe casino model and (7) completed set.

the truth in every way you can – and then they'll forgive you when you're lying." (Not that the staff of the Mozart Museum in Salzburg did: when they found out I was involved with the film of *that* terrible play which insulted the memory of the great composer, they literally manhandled me out of the door...) The gaudy finery of the mourners who appear at Mozart's funeral, for example, is not authentic. But the image of these characters in mud-spattered purple (Milos made the actors stomp around in the mud for an hour before shooting), their feathered headgear dripping with rain, was so much more memorable than reality (heavy black weeds were worn for such occasions).

I always look for projects which are different to what I've done before. I've made it a point to cover all the genres. I also want to work with directors who have some integrity and originality, and are willing to trust me. Good design happens when you work with a director who has a strong vision. One has to be prepared to adapt one's approach to different directors. Milos likes to work from research and photographs. Mike Nichols is very big on verbal process. Brian De Palma, a tireless and wonderful film communicator, transforms his location Polaroids into stick-figure storyboards. My personal bias is against the classic painted set illustration. It's static – the antithesis of our medium, which is about creating a three-dimensional, fluid world: moving pictures. So I'm always on the lookout for alternative tools to express my ideas. Recently, I've fallen in love with the new tiny, compact video cameras: I can use them to shoot inside my models, whooshing through them. It gives the director a real idea of

the possibilities. One thing I always do on a film is to create a "bible" containing the fabrics for the soft furnishings and costumes, the colours for walls and floors and for the gels in the lights. I design this "bible" so that when you open it out, you can see the visual development of the whole film from beginning to end.

It's important to remember that film-making is a communal enterprise. Designers and D.P.s are like apples and oranges; our work is completely interdependent. The design concept has to include what the cinematographer is thinking about or it's not going to work. I wouldn't dream of using a colour on a set that I hadn't discussed prior to shooting. The process is about continually checking back and forth with the D.P. and the director throughout the shoot. Research and design do not end after pre-production; circumstances and emphases change when shooting begins. I always go to rushes – that's how I see which ideas are working strongly, and which ones I can discard.

I would say that the one indispensable quality a production designer must have is the ability to observe, and to be able to translate what you observe into story terms. You have to be curious about the world: how things are made, how they are put together. Everything else can be learned – but that has to be in you.

biography

The son of a screenwriter, Starski grew up near Poland's biggest studio in Lodz. After studying fine arts, he began working in the art department. In 1975, he designed **The Shadow Line**, his first film for Andrzej Wajda. Although renowned for changing his key personnel from film to film, Wajda kept faith with his young designer, continuing their collaboration on films such as **Man of Marble** (1976), **The**

allan starski

Young Ladies of Wilko (1979), **The Conductor** (1979), **Man of Iron** (1981), **Danton** (1982), **Korczak** (1990), **Holy Week** (1996) and **Pan Tadeusz** (1999). He has designed in all over 60 films, including **No End** (1984, Krzysztof Kieslowski), **Daens** (1992, Stijn Coninx), **Europa, Europa** (1991) and **Washington Square** (1997) for director Agnieszka Holland. Despite twice having the opportunity to go to Hollywood – after working with Alan Pakula in pre-production of **Sophie's Choice**, and then following the Oscar for his work on **Schindler's List** (1993, Steven Spielberg), Starski remains based in Poland, in order to work with Wajda and other European directors. "We must fight for bigger films in Europe," he believes, "not only for the small productions which can be 'designed' by a location manager and set decorator; otherwise the craft of production design will die here."

interview

I was five when I first set foot on a movie set in the Lodz film studio. They were shooting a war film, and although I was very impressed by all the dramatic scenes with Nazis, what made the deepest impression on me was opening the door to one of the shops in a street constructed on the back-lot and finding that there was nothing behind it...

How does one define the work of a production designer? Sometimes people say, OK, you are doing a contemporary story, what's the big deal, all you have to do is copy reality. But this is absolutely false thinking. Film stories, even when they are taken from life, are fictions. The designer's responsibility is to make the audience believe that the artifice they are watching is real. Through the medium of a set, our job is to impart essential information to reinforce that belief: where are we? In what time period? What does this setting mean for the characters? How does it relate to the story? When I think about the establishing shot of a new set, I

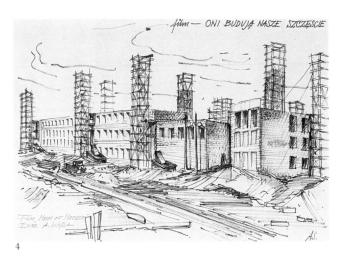

(1–7) **Man of Marble**: (1) Starski with Wajda: "I had the feeling that we were creating something politically important. The whole crew knew the film went way beyond the limits imposed by the censor. It challenged the Communist system." (3) Starski found the former sculptor of Soviet statuary to carve the statue of the film's protagonist – a bricklayer transformed into "hero of the people" before coming into conflict with the state. (2) Actor Jerzy Radziwilowicz with his statue. (4–7) Starski had to research and recreate the bricklaying event (the Russian method of using concrete blocks had long superseded the old building method).

imagine it as a film poster in which one is trying to communicate all this information with great immediacy and clarity; while also evoking the atmosphere of the film and its aesthetic sensibility.

I choose a project not on the basis of the script or the genre of the film, but because of who the director is. He (or she) is ultimately responsible for the vision of the film, and therefore will have a strong influence on my work. It was an incredible honour when Andrzej Wajda asked me to work with him for the first time – to me he was a living legend, whose films were artistic and political events. Some directors simply expect the designer to reproduce every detail of their vision on the screen; they don't welcome any kind of contribution or collaboration. Wajda is a joy to work with. A former art student himself, his ability to make rapid sketches to describe a scene or a shot makes it easy to grasp his aesthetic ideas, but he always remains open to other people's ideas. Likewise Steven Spielberg; although he had always prepared his productions in meticulous detail with storyboards, he sacrificed this method for **Schindler's List** in order to achieve greater realism. As a result, he gave me real freedom, encouraging me to surprise him with a new set or location, in order that he could look at it with the eye of someone who had just arrived to shoot a documentary. This made the film a fantastic challenge for me.

Often, people say to me, OK, you've done so many movies from the 19th century, it must make it easy for you. But although I am familiar with the period, each time it is a

different location, a different director, a different movie. I approach every film I work on as a new adventure which demands its own aesthetic response. When I begin to work on a film, my priority is to try to understand how the director wants to approach the story. Is it going to be played naturalistically? Or with irony? Or exaggerated? Once I know, I can follow this tone in each set I design. When I worked with Wajda on **Danton**, we asked ourselves, "what does the idea of revolution mean to us?" We thought about our experience of totalitarianism in Poland; the brutality and violence which the uncompromising pursuit of power brings. We remembered how the Communist administration divided once-beautiful palaces into rows of box-like offices for the army of bureaucrats. We applied this to our recreation of Paris after the French Revolution. A good screenplay also helps me to flesh out the design concept, particularly when the characters are well described, and they have some kind of individuality beyond their function in the plot. In **Danton**, the contrast between the two central protagonists was fascinating. Danton was a kind of playboy of his time, a sensualist and aesthete who collected beautiful objects, whereas Robespierre was a martinet, very ascetic and puritanical. If the screenplay is based on a novel, like **Washington Square**, it can be invaluable to go back to the source material – particularly with an author like Henry James, who writes about all the small details.

Research is one of my most important tools. I collect anything and everything relating to the period – books, drawings, photographs. Often this material throws up something

1

2

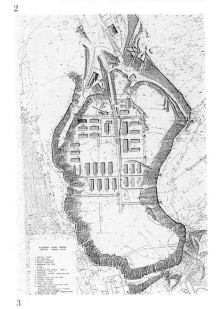

3

4

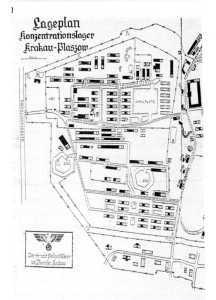

5

6

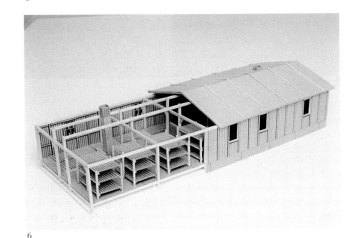

7

(1–15) **Schindler's List**: (1) Reference photograph of Plaszow forced labour camp. (2) Original SS plan of camp used as research and (3) Starski's adaptation of it. (4–5) Model and still of camp. (6–7) Model and still of barrack with triple-tiered bunks. SS Kommandant Amon Goeth's villa: (8) interior elevation; (9) dressed set prior to shooting; (10) Ralph Fiennes and Liam Neeson in a scene shot on the set; (11) model of villa; (12) construction of villa in studio and (13) exterior of villa. (14–15) "I felt the story had to be real. The camera should not be restricted by design; it should be able to move anywhere as if in a documentary."

interesting or unusual which I will show to the director. On **Korczak**, I collected photographs of the period (the Nazi occupation of Warsaw and the Jewish ghetto), from which Wajda and I then made a selection to determine the atmosphere for the film. I also look at paintings of the period to help me create an appropriate colour palette. Researching a film about Franz Schubert, however, I found that every painting of 1820s' Vienna made the city look almost too perfect. I met up with a historian who told me that the artists of the time were under strict censorship; they were not allowed to depict the city as it really was with its run-down areas and poverty. When doing the research, one must never forget the dramatic requirements of the film. Designing the factory set for **Schindler's List**, Spielberg asked me for big windows in Schindler's office overlooking the plant, so that it might appear to the workers below like a kind of paradise with the beautiful secretaries as angels. It was a great idea, so I didn't hesitate to throw out the research which informed me that such windows in fact would have been much smaller. One should never allow oneself to become a slave to one's research. The same rule applies when you bring in a specialist to help you achieve some period detail or furnishing; it's no good if they are not prepared to be flexible and adapt their knowledge to the needs of the film.

Location scouting with the director is a very important part of the collaborative process. New ideas are suggested by interesting locations which might improve the dramatic construction of a scene. Even when the director doesn't like a location that I have proposed, it can be very useful to me; as

he explains why it's not right, it helps me to understand his concept better. Once we have established the main locations for the film, it gives us a physical foundation for the film's look. I habitually take panoramic photographs of each of the locations which I then stick down in the order they appear in the script to see how they will work together. The first three minutes of **The Shadow Line** (my first film for Wajda) featured shots taken in three different countries – and yet it had to look like one seamless scene in one location (conversely, when we shot **Europa, Europa**, the Polish locations had to suggest three countries – Poland, Germany and Russia). As a designer, I like to work on movies which combine studio and location shooting. The challenge for me is to integrate them aesthetically in such a way that the audience cannot tell the difference. I have to know that I will be able to adapt a chosen location so that it will conform with the film's aesthetic. It's no good if we find a beautiful palace and then the owner tells us we can't change anything.

Only when the main locations have been selected do I begin to draw. For me, the most important elements in any set are the proportions and dimensions. I find it essential to do a scale plan which ensures that the spatial relationships are correct (in a sketch, you can cheat the perspective, make things look bigger or smaller). For example, I always pay a lot of attention to doorways, because actors enter and exit through them and often stand in or near them. If there are important details such as a fireplace or a door handle, I will draw them as well. While I am drawing, I also think about how the design will interact with the cinematography. There is

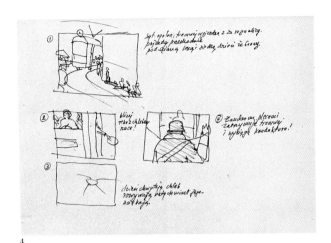

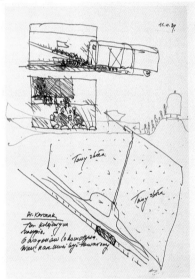

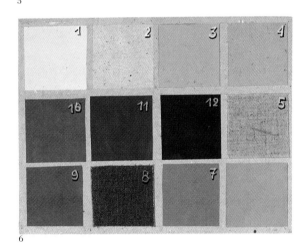

(1–6) **Korczak**: (1) "I collected many photographs of the Warsaw ghetto and went through them with Wajda, making choices for the film's atmosphere." (2, 4) "Wajda often sketches his ideas for scenes or shots. These visual anecdotes make it much easier for me to grasp the director's practical and aesthetic ideas, before I begin to think about space, proportions and dimensions." (5) Starski's illustration. (6) Part of the designer's palette for the film: because it was shot in black and white, tonal separation and texturing of surfaces were of critical importance.

1

2

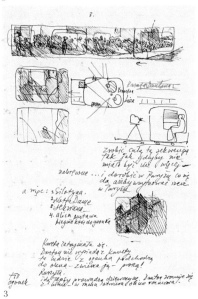

3

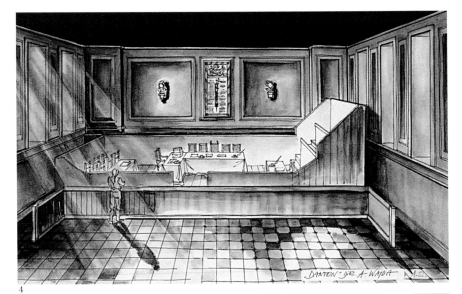

4

5

6

7

8

9

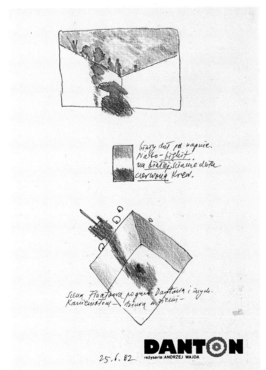

10

11

Martial law was declared in Starski's native Poland before production began on **Danton** (1–11). The visualisation of the French Revolution reflected the film-maker's experience of Communism. The palaces of the *ancien régime* were turned into partitioned offices for the new bureaucracy and revolutionary army. Interiors were stripped of their lavish decor and replaced by utilitarian furniture made from wood planks. Against this background, the film's action portrayed Danton struggling against the new state he himself had helped to create. (2) The Ten Commandments of the Revolution designed for the courtroom; (3) Wajda's sketches; (4) Starski's drawing of courtroom; (5) Danton in the courtroom and (6) Robespierre *(far right)* modelling for David in the sculptor's studio. (8) Rather than hire a guillotine from a conventional props rental, Starski created one which was closer to the design style of the film and which would better express the drama of the story. (9) Guillotined corpses in pit. (10) Sketches for the low- and high-angle shots of Danton's corpse when thrown into the pit, with symbolic use of colours of the tricolour French flag.

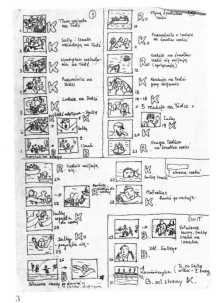

(1–4) **Europa, Europa:** To find the elite SS school where the film's Jewish protagonist becomes a star student, Starski recce'd school buildings throughout formerly German regions of Poland. He found nothing that coincided with the style of the film, which aimed to reflect the extravagance and megalomania of both Nazism and Stalinism. Then he hit upon the inspired idea of setting the school scenes in Warsaw's Palace of Culture and Science, a colossus from the Soviet era. "In the vast, pompous interiors I found what I was looking for. Although it was built for an opposing ideology, it shared the same aesthetic." Starski added the Nazi decoration, including the sub-aqua swastika in the swimming pool. (3) Storyboard by director Agnieszka Holland and (4) design sketch for podium.

2

often conflict between designers and D.P.s which happens because they work in isolation from each other. On my first film as an assistant art director, I was very fortunate to meet and work with Witold Sobocinski, the best D.P. in Poland at the time. He taught me a lot about the relationship between our respective crafts which has greatly influenced how I approach my work. I learned to think about interesting ways to characterise the light source – for example, by layering the set so that you can see through several rooms, with a window in the distant background. I also like to discuss with the D.P. what kind of light he wants to use (hard or soft, warm or cold) and also what film stocks and which processes. These inevitably affect the colours in the design. In **Danton**, we knew we wanted the actors' faces to look weary, pale with exhaustion. To achieve this, some colour had to be lost in the labs when the film was printed. As a result, all the warm colours became colder. I had to compensate for this, otherwise all my walls would have looked blue. This was particularly important because I associated blue with Robespierre and intended to use the colour only once in the film – in his apartment.

As production designers, we have to remember that the essential difference between what we do, and what a theatre designer does, is the camera. If I know that one set is going to be used for two weeks' shooting, I try to design it in such a way that the crew won't run out of ideas for coverage after three days. I create opportunities for interesting camera angles and movement, and I populate the set with possibilities for visual anecdotes. Sometimes these relate to leitmotifs running through the entire film, like the Nazi and Communist symbols in **Europa, Europa**. Sometimes they are designed to provide interesting background action – for example, a scene in **Danton** where bureaucrats are seen through doorways making inventories of objects confiscated from the aristocracy, while sleeping guards can be glimpsed slumped in their chairs. Good props also have anecdotal value, which is why I like them to be very realistic and precise. Often I will design them myself rather than going to a props-hire facility. After looking at prints and paintings from the period of **Danton**, I knew that if I filtered this research through my imagination, I could create a more interesting guillotine for the film than I'd ever be able to hire.

The most important moment for me on a film is not when I show the director my drawings or models, but when I take him on to the completed set for the first time; it's only at this moment that you know truly whether your work is good. It's so exciting when you see the director is genuinely inspired by what you've given him. I don't believe the importance of our work should be exaggerated, however. When you see the edited film, it's possible that a lot of one's work is not seen – shots and even whole scenes may have been cut. In the final analysis, the film is more important than the design. You have to love movies to be a production designer, and you must be able to understand your place in the process. You have to be able to distinguish between the ideas it's essential to fight for, and those you can let go of. This understanding can only come from a combination of artistic knowledge and practical experience.

biography

The daughter of a Swedish politician, Anna Asp grew up in an environment devoid of culture. In Stockholm, however, she gradually discovered her vocation as a production designer. She collaborated with Ingmar Bergman in the twilight of his feature film career, designing **Autumn Sonata** (1978) and **Fanny & Alexander** (1984, for which she won an Academy Award), as well as his television film, **After the Rehearsal**

anna asp

(1983). Subsequently, she designed Andrei Tarkovsky's last film **The Sacrifice** (1986), before embarking on her long-standing collaboration with Danish director Bille August. Their first film together was **Pelle the Conqueror** (1987), after which they took on Bergman's screenplay **The Best Intentions** (1992); based on the story of the Bergman's parents, the material had a direct connection with the story of **Fanny & Alexander**. Asp and August have continued to work together, on **The House of the Spirits** (1993), **Jerusalem** (1996), **Smilla's Sense of Snow** (1997) and **Les Misérables** (1998).

interview

After school, I worked as a secretary in Stockholm. It was the most boring, depressing job, so I decided that I had to do something which would be more fun before I thought about getting married and settling down. I was accepted into Stockholm's school of photography (where Bille August was a fellow student). Although I had no ambitions to be a production designer at the time, studying stills photography turned out to be an ideal background for my future career. I learned how to think in terms of composition – how one constructs a frame through contrasting colour values, or in black and white, through tonal separation. While I was a student, I also designed my first set – for a theatre production. This experience gave me my first taste of working in three dimensions with people who were constantly in motion (as opposed to the frozen moment of a still). After my photography course, I was accepted to study design in the newly-opened film school. I don't know how much the course helped me; the school was so poorly-equipped when I first

production design & art direction

Asp's method is to relate sets and furnishings to characters. (1–6) **Fanny & Alexander**: the grandmother's house reflected the notion that she was a prima donna of the stage. The sets (1, 4–5) were about power and theatricality. The bishop's house (2) evoked his austere, Puritan nature – a prison for the children. The home of the cabalistic puppet-maker Jacobi (3), by contrast, represented to the children escape and enchantment. Asp, who involves herself in every detail of set dressing, learned from Bergman to place furniture in the middle of the room so the camera is able to move freely around it.

arrived, I couldn't even find a pencil! Furthermore, it was the late-'60s, and we seemed to spend most of our time in meetings so that even the smallest decision could be made democratically. But by then, my experience of photography and theatre had already given me a solid background.

By a stroke of good fortune, my graduation from film school coincided with the moment that Swedish film-makers returned to shooting in the studio, a practise abandoned during a decade of working on location in order to attain greater realism. I heard that Ingmar Bergman was about to produce a television serial, so I wrote to him asking for a job... To my amazement, he wrote back, and we met up, and I became an employee of his company, working initially as a set decorator on several Bergman productions. It was a very disciplined environment, and everyone followed his work methods, which included extensive preparation. Before each production, we would have to shoot tests of the actors' faces against whichever colours and fabrics we intended to use, in different lighting conditions. From these tests, we'd select the combinations which worked best. I learned to avoid blue, which registers much brighter on film than to the naked eye, especially if the film is printed less red to take some colour out of the actors' faces. This experience helped me to realise that the audience should be more focused on the actors rather than the design. To this end, I have always sought to make the colour of the walls in my sets darker than the tone of skin, so that on film, the face stands out from the background. Working in Bergman's company also taught me about what the camera required for a scene to be effective. For example, by

positioning the furniture in the middle of the room, it gives the actors and camera something to move around, as opposed to being stuck in a corner where the options for staging are limited.

As a designer, I prefer period films to contemporary subjects. I find working with the past gives me more scope because I can be more objective about the world. With a contemporary film, there's no distance and the danger is that your decisions can be too easily influenced by personal taste ("oh, I like that sofa") rather than what is good for the film. I like to be able to create a whole world on the screen. My starting point is the script. I am not concerned so much with how the writer has described the story's settings, as with who the characters are. A really good script, like **Fanny & Alexander**, for example, makes my job much easier. The characters immediately evoked their settings in my mind. The grandmother was the "queen", a great prima donna of the theatre. Her environment had to suggest power and theatricality. By contrast, the apartment of her son Oscar, his wife Emilie, and their children Fanny and Alexander needed to feel airier and lighter, whereas the house of the bishop whom Emilie marries after Oscar's premature death was clearly a prison for the children. Similarly, in **The House of the Spirits**, Clara's ancestral home represented the "old world", suggesting not only her female qualities but the ghosts of previous generations of the family. Esteban's hacienda, meanwhile, represented the forces of the new world, fascistic, very masculine. If this sense of character isn't implicit in the script, it's more difficult to create an environment that will

1

2

5

6

7

3

4

8

9

10

11

12

13

14

(1–14) **The Best Intentions**: The priest's house in the north of Sweden (3–7) is very characteristic of the houses Asp loves to design. In its rural isolation it is always seen in the context of nature and the changing seasons. It also features a "face" on its façade (7), while the placement of Christ on the Crucifix and the adjacent crosses in the window frames evoke Golgotha (5). Models (3–4) play a vital role in Asp's design process. She applies paint colours that match the colours she will use in the final set, and she experiments with lighting: "When the set is constructed on the stage, it's like walking into my model." (8–9) The sanatorium bedroom set. (10–11) Location for kitchen set, before and after. Vermeer's use of light was an important inspiration for Asp while developing the film's look. (12–14) The summer house set was influenced by the classical minimalism of Finnish architect Eliel Saarinen.

resonate with the story. When I designed the mechanic's home in **Smilla's Sense of Snow**, I was lost. The script revealed nothing about his character – his secretive nature was never sufficiently developed to reveal what he might be hiding. Designing in such circumstances becomes like creating a set for a commercial – it is about form rather than content.

I always create "bibles" for each of the principal characters – collages which feature colours, shapes and fabrics or other textures through which I can relate design to character. I also do sketches for myself detailing the main view of the set. This allows me to begin to get an idea of proportions and angles, and where the light comes from. However, models rather than drawings are my most important tool when I design a set. A model, because it is three-dimensional, gives a much more immediate impression of the atmosphere of the set. I can put light through the windows at different angles. I can also get much closer to the colours we'll use in the finished set than I can on a drawing. I take great care over all the details of the model, so when people walk on the set, it's like walking into the model. Because it is so precise, it allows the director to see exactly what I intend to do, which means that if he wants to change something, it can be done before the set is built. It's very important that the director feels at home in the sets I give him, because they are where he is going to create his film. When I worked with Andrei Tarkovsky on **The Sacrifice**, the house which is the film's central location evolved through our conversations. He wanted to discuss every detail, for example the distance between the top of a chair to the sill of a window. When I showed him the scale plan of the interior, he

introduced me to a device he used to enable him to determine on the plan what would be seen by the camera from any given position, with a lens of any given focal length. It was a revelation to me, helping me to visualise much more precisely how a set might be used in relation to camera composition and blocking of the actors. Working with Tarkovsky on the house taught me another valuable lesson about film-making. The exterior had to be constructed in relation to the trees we planted outside. Because they were not particularly tall, it restricted the height of the house. We began to realise that the scale of the interior (which we built in the studio) was more than twice the size of the exterior. We agonised about whether this would be a problem; but ultimately, no one who saw the finished film commented on it. Most people believe that theatre (a three-dimensional medium with real people) is fake, whereas film (images projected on a flat screen) is somehow more realistic. But it's quite incredible what you can get away with on film.

I have constructed a lot of houses for films I've designed, and I try to think of them as characters in their own right. I like to play with the idea of making a face out of the façade of a house. In **The Sacrifice**, I designed one side of the house with two windows resembling eyes and a door for the mouth. We came to think of it as "God's face". The hacienda in **The House of the Spirits**, whose owner Esteban struck me as a kind of Nazi, was deliberately designed like a skull with two black holes for the eyes and four black teeth. For **Pelle the Conqueror**, I felt the house should feel like a prison; I constructed the walls and painted them black and white,

(1–7) **The Sacrifice**: The house evolved from long and detailed conversations between Asp and director Tarkovsky. It was designed to be timeless: "the film could have been set in the 19th century or in the future at the time of some nuclear catastrophe" (by uncanny coincidence the disaster of Chernobyl happened shortly after the film's production). (1) The location on Faro. (2) Model of the house – "God's face" on façade. (3–4) Construction of the house and (5) its destruction at the end of the film. (6) Asp's model in front of the completed house. (7) The interior of the house was four times larger than the exterior; Tarkovsky and Asp took a gamble that no one would notice.

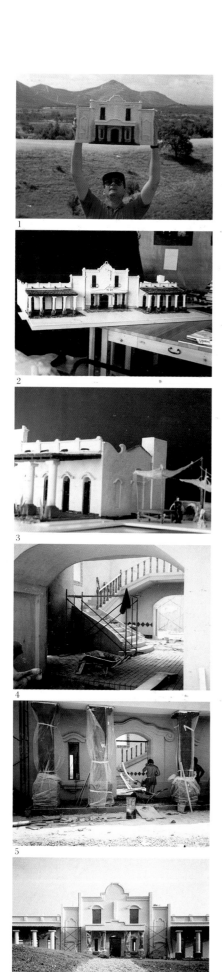

(1–13) **The House of the Spirits**: Asp's process begins with making "bibles" for different characters – collages of fabrics, colours, textures, shapes, references – which are then translated into sets. (7) "Bible" for Esteban: Asp viewed the character as a macho, "new world" Fascist, and the design of the hacienda interior (8) – "very square, very masculine" – reflects this. Asp's model of the hacienda photographed against the landscape and villa construction (1–6). Asp's "face" on the façade of Esteban's home, resembled a skull.

9

11

12

10

13

In contrast to Esteban's masculine decor, Clara's "bible" (9) and home embody her feminine nature, and also her connection with the past, with the "old world" of her ancestors. It is filled with family heirlooms, rounded shapes, plants, drapes and mirrors. Where Esteban's hacienda is sparse and sombre, Clara's environment is cluttered, but full of light and reflective surfaces (10–13).

Jerusalem: (1) Asp's design sketch for Via Dolorosa. (2–3) Location snapshot by Asp used as a basis for the design of the harbour. (4-6) **Les Misérables**: Construction of the Paris street set in Barrandov Studio, Prague.

while keeping the inner yard devoid of any vegetation. The relationship between the house and its setting is also important to me. I always like to be involved in finding the locations, because it's vital that they belong to the world you are trying to create for the film. In **Pelle the Conqueror**, the prison-like atmosphere of the home, I felt, should be in contrast with the beautiful countryside beyond, the lush, rolling hills where Pelle could feel free. I think a lot about the seasons in which the film is unfolding, because they can yield rich visual and dramatic possibilities. **Pelle the Conqueror** featured scenes shot in summer and in winter; for the former, we had everyone dressed in light colours, and in winter, they were dressed in black, which made them stand out starkly against the snow. It's also important to take into account what kind of light the location will have when you're shooting – what direction it's coming from, as well as its intensity. I find the north European light much easier to work with than the Mediterranean light we had on **The House of the Spirits** (shot mostly in Portugal), where I constructed the hacienda to take advantage of the amazing landscape around it. However, such was the dazzling intensity of the light when we shot the film, it was impossible to see anything through the windows.

I am always involved with the furnishings and props. I don't select the actors' hand-props, but I design or pick almost everything else myself, in order to ensure that the textures and colours are in harmony with the design scheme. For the same reason, I like to be able to collaborate with the costume designer, but this can be difficult to achieve in practical terms. On **Les Misérables**, for example, I was working in

Prague while Gabriella Pescucci, the costume designer, was working in London and New York. This is perhaps typical of bigger productions; but ideally you want to have enough time together so that you can adjust your work to each other. Working on **Les Misérables**, however, gave me the opportunity to work with computer-generated imagery for the first time, in order to extend the wall of Paris and build up the city skyline behind it. It was a fascinating experience, but I have to confess to mixed feelings about CGI. One can envisage a day when new technology makes the work of the production designer redundant. However, if it is used in connection with traditional methods, the computer is a tool which allows you to achieve things which you cannot construct on the stage. On a personal level, though, it doesn't really interest me; I like to work in three dimensions, I like the physicality of a set or a model. I like to be able to reach out and touch it.

To anyone thinking about a career as a production designer, I'd say, don't do it – unless you're prepared to make sacrifices. It's not the kind of job you can do on a nine-to-five basis, which makes it difficult to combine with a normal life. You have to be obsessed by film and design to be a production designer. It's very hard work – but it can also be a lot of fun.

A true Renaissance man, Hobbs combines his work as a production designer with portraiture, sculpture and plaster-work, interior decoration and exhibition design. He began his career as a props-maker before entering the film industry, providing sculpture and special effects for Ken Russell (on such films as **The Devils** and **Savage Messiah**), storyboards for Terry Gilliam (on **The Time Bandits**) and was involved

christopher hobbs

in the production of Derek Jarman's early Super-8mm films. He designed nearly all Jarman's feature films: **Jubilee** (1977), **Caravaggio** (1986), **The Last of England** (1987), **Aria** (segment, 1987), **The Garden** (1990, which he co-designed) and **Edward II** (1991). He designed **Gothic** (1986) and **Salome's Last Dance** (1988) for Ken Russell, **The Long Day Closes** (1992) and **The Neon Bible** (1995) for Terence Davies, **Velvet Goldmine** (1998) for Todd Haynes and **Mansfield Park** (1999) for Patricia Rozema. He has also designed pop videos and television drama (the *Comic Strip*, Dennis Potter's *Cold Lazarus* and *Gormanghast*). He is a hands-on designer who dresses his own sets and whose knowledge of optics enables him to create in-camera special effects for his films. His work – particularly on films such as **Edward II** – demonstrates how limited resources can be the mother of invention, and in its stylisation also offers an alternative approach to film than the virtual realism of so much contemporary cinema.

interview

I had no great ambition to get into the film industry, nor to become a designer as such. I always wanted to be an artist. I taught myself to paint by going to galleries and copying the Old Masters, and also by apprenticing myself briefly to a picture restorer, learning how pictures are constructed physically. All art is firstly about observation, and then about acquiring the skills to transform observation into art. This background indirectly stood me in good stead for my future career; you can learn a lot about composition and lighting from a painter like Caravaggio. I also gained a very simple knowledge of optics through studying how painters create the illusion of reality through *trompe l'oeil* and forced perspective. Film designers, like painters, are illusionists; people forget that what's on the screen is not three-dimensional reality – it's actually just a flat pattern of lights. So if you learn to manipulate that pattern, you can deceive your audience into believing that what you're showing them is real. It's all lies; everything you see on film is lies.

1

2

3

4

5

6

7

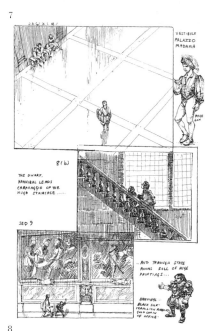

8

9

(1–15) **Caravaggio**: (1–3) Hobbs recreated all the paintings in the film himself: "We couldn't use reproductions of the originals because they were in such bad condition – there was no way we could make an audience believe they were newly-painted." The film evolved over seven years; initially it was envisaged on a lavish budget. (4–9) "I did elaborate storyboards to show backers what the film would look like." It was finally produced on a very low budget. (10–13) The grandeur of his original story-boards is replaced in the final production sketches by an emphasis on simplicity, line and texture, with selected props, furnishings and costumes evoking the period.

(1–8) **Edward II**: In this film, Hobbs pushed the simplicity of **Caravaggio** towards abstraction. The main set featured two ramps, five blocks, and a surrounding wall in two sections. (2) Hobbs' portrait of Tilda Swinton waiting for a take on the set. (4–5) Details of set and wall texture. (6–8) The only other set on the film was the cast-iron dungeon, influenced by Dante Ferretti's engine room for **And the Ship Sails On** (see p 55) and the pit in Poe's story 'The Pit and the Pendulum'.

I was about 19 when I realised I wasn't going to be able to make a living from painting, and so I joined a firm in Covent Garden which made stage props for all the big West End shows. It was a perfect training; I reckon I learned more than any design course could have taught me. I made everything from jewelled hatpins to the Lord Mayor's coach, portrait busts of Frankie Howard to monsters. I had to be able to make anything on demand to a deadline for a budget. If I only had half-a-crown to make a diamond brooch, I'd have to work out the cheapest way of doing it. This later helped me as a production designer, because a vital part of the job on any film is to look at how much money you have to spend and be able to relate it to what you want to put on the screen. Sometimes, the cheapest way to do something can also be the best; for example, if I have to gild something on a film, I never use gold leaf. It's expensive; moreover, the cheap alternative – gold foil, such as you find in chocolate bars – actually looks better on film. I still make props today; I have busy fingers, and love inventing things (as a child, I was profoundly influenced by the work of Heath-Robinson). I try to make something for every film I work on, partly to keep me sane. I'll often wander around the markets and buy things for no good reason other than it might get used in a film one day. For instance, I bought a swordfish's snout, so like a real steel blade in design, and decided it needed a handle. I made one and decorated it with Arab jewels and snakeskins – an extraordinary object, completely meaningless, but which I used in **Cold Lazarus** as a kind of futuristic antique.

In the late-'60s, I began my collaboration with Derek Jarman.

His first directorial efforts were really improvisations with a Super-8mm camera and a bunch of friends jumping about with paper bags on their heads; I was the person who supplied the paper bags. The first proper film was **Jubilee** which again wasn't serious design – just emptying skips of rubbish on to warehouse floors; but there was a great sense of camaraderie and fun, which continued even as the films grew in scale and ambition. **Caravaggio** remains the most enjoyable experience I've had. It was not at all like shooting a proper film; more like a bunch of friends and enthusiasts bashing together to make something in appalling conditions (I remember Sandy Powell making the costumes in a disused lavatory). The film was the result of seven years' work for both Derek and me. Initially, it was supposed to be a grandiose epic, shot in Italian palaces; but as deal after deal failed to materialise, the budget dwindled to a teeny-weeny BFI grant. We had no choice but to make the design very simple. The approach to **Caravaggio** was to make the backgrounds very sparse, and spend what money we had on the props. If we needed a shiny marble floor to say "this is a grand palace", I'd cover the concrete floor with water, which gave the right effect on film (although the poor actor had to sit with his toes in water).

It was only after being forced to think simply that I began to realise that simplicity is actually by far the best way of going about things (whatever the size of the budget). Fellini has always been a great influence on me, because he often used wonderfully simple ideas with elaborate textures. On **Edward II**, we took the approach even further, simplifying the design

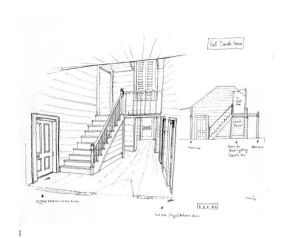

1

2

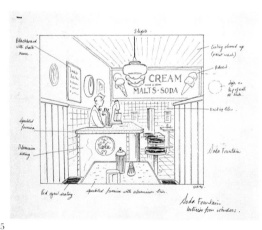

3

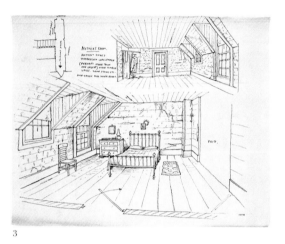

4

5

7

8

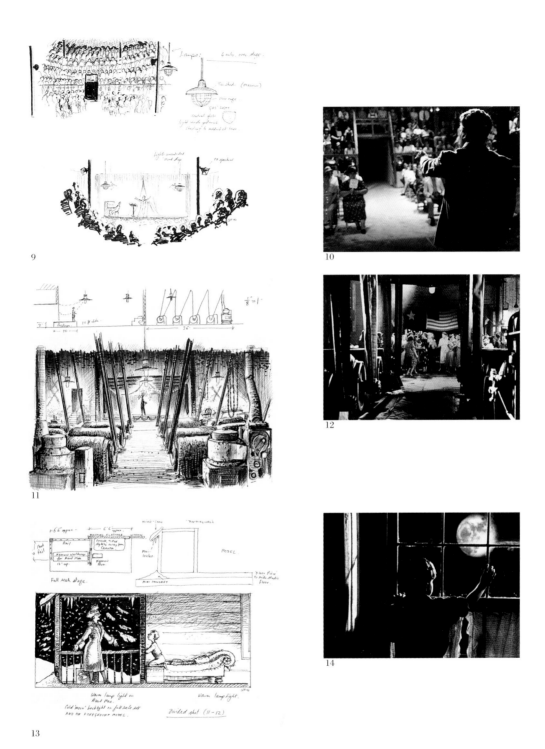

9

10

11

12

13

14

(1–14) **The Neon Bible**: (1–4) David's house – hallway and mother's room. (5) Interior diner sketch. (7) Exterior movie theatre sketch. "I lived in Alabama as a child in the '50s, so I had a feeling for the atmosphere – peeling paint, rotting floorboards – which was bolstered by hunting for props in Atlanta markets and looking at painters like Rockwell and Hopper." (8) Hobbs' use of "a very Hopper red." (9–10) Prayer meeting set. (11–12) Interior of the textile factory. (13–14) Interior/exterior of David's room and porch: "The script called for these strange transitions and it was up to me to make them happen in a way that was simultaneously realistic and magical, as when David's voice-over says 'there was no snow that winter', but you're seeing snow fall before your eyes."

to the point of abstraction. Although I'm a figurative painter, I love abstract shapes and textures. The experience taught me how little is needed to create an image on film. There was a scene in which Mortimer refers to "This ragged banner which has led us through battle". Derek and I discussed what sort of banner we should have, eagles or lions rampant, etc. We quickly realised that whatever we chose might look mock-medieval and potentially undermine the film's look; so I said, "well, do we actually need to see it?" It was in the dialogue, the character was looking up at it – but it didn't necessarily need to be in the shot. So there was no banner, just the allusion which enabled the audience to imagine their own banner. In practice, this is what happens when you read a book; the reader imagines the scene described by the author. In the same way, in film, all you need is a pointed arch in shadow to imply a Gothic or medieval building. You don't necessarily need to show the entire building. It's a lesson I've applied again and again – in **The Neon Bible**, the audience thinks it has seen a steam train; in reality all it's seen is a plywood box painted black and a lot of steam... Shadows, reactions and suggestion can be so much more powerful than showing everything explicitly.

As a designer I'm drawn to period films with a touch of fantasy, or pure fantasy, or science fiction; probably because my childhood imagination was bound up with the past and future much more than the present. I'd also always rather work with directors like Derek or Terence Davies who are passionate about what they do rather than somebody who's just doing it for the money. It's my job to give the director what he or she wants, but at the same time I have to serve the script. It can be a delicate balance, but if you jettison the script, you can find yourself getting drawn into things that are quite wrong. After reaching an understanding with the director, I go off into my own space and build up an image of the film in my head. I try to emulate Wittgenstein's Martian and see the world as if for the first time; unburdened by preconceptions or clichés, I avoid referring to other films. Viewed this way, the ordinary becomes quite magical. I look for things to bolster my image of the film but I'm always aware, when I'm researching a period film, that what is in the books represents only what happens to have survived. There are huge dollops of the past we know nothing about – because even if you're doing a film set 30 years ago, it's amazing how much has been forgotten. When I did **The Long Day Closes**, which was based on memories of Terence Davies' childhood, there were no photographs to work from (his family didn't have a camera), and so I sat down with him and pieced together what his Liverpool home looked like. From the clues he gave me, we worked out it was early 19th century, and then with my knowledge of that period's architecture and some additional research, I was able to gain a better picture, which in turn enabled him to remember details; a doily on the sideboard, for example, which he'd forgotten. Ultimately, I knew I'd got it right because when he walked on to the set, his first response was, "It's much smaller than I remember" – which is what everyone says when they go back to a childhood place.

My rule of thumb on a period film is that if somebody who lived at the time saw my representation of it, they shouldn't be

1

2

3

4

5

6

7

8

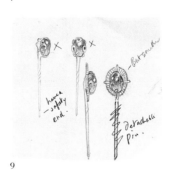

9

(1–9) **Velvet Goldmine**: (1–3) Painted glass shot with scenic painting behind for opening sequence of the film. (4) Hobbs' original illustration for scenic painting. (5–6) The living-room in Arthur Stuart's childhood home in Liverpool and (7) sofa designs and fabrics used in the set. (8–9) Hobbs' Oscar Wilde pin: "I try to make one prop on every film I do – to keep myself sane!"

1

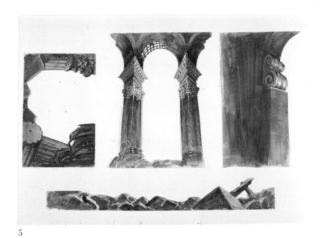

3

4

5

6

2

(1–6) **Velvet Goldmine**: (1–2) Sketch and still of the interior of St Francis Hotel. (3–6) "Director Todd Haynes wanted a ruined ballroom with a staircase and chandelier; clearly we couldn't afford to build it as a full-scale set because it would have been vast, and we felt CGI wouldn't give us the look we wanted. So I said, this isn't reality, it's a dream within a dream, so let's do it like grand opera, with old-fashioned *trompe l'oeil* style painting on flats. The scenic painters weren't used to the style; I painted the set myself in the end."

shocked. I did a film set in the 1840s and found out that there were steam vehicles at the time. Knowing the technology existed, I invented one for the film. Likewise, I knew that at the time in which **Mansfield Park** was written, automata were very popular; when director Patricia Rozema asked me for a prop to symbolise slavery (a theme of the novel), I invented a slave-boy automaton to light Sir Thomas' cigars. **Mansfield Park** also called for me to design a slum, the heroine Fanny's childhood home. The picturesque way poverty is depicted in 18th- and 19th-century drama has become a cliché which I wanted to avoid. I tried to find out what poor people who couldn't afford paint did to decorate their homes, and learned that they'd use blood (mixed with lime) from the pig slaughtered in winter and paint their homes red. This detail not only enabled me to do something different, but also served to make Fanny's home appear womb-like and welcoming, in contrast to the coldness of **Mansfield Park**. One should never seek to recreate a period – one should attempt to reinvent it. The primary function of design in film is to comment on and boost what's in the story. It is a theatrical medium. One telling detail in how a set or location is dressed can suffice to evoke a whole period. In **Velvet Goldmine**, I used a single icon to create the illusion of 1970s' King's Road on location in 1990s Portobello Road – the Red Indian painted face in the window of the boutique named Granny Takes A Trip.

I begin sketching as soon as I've read the script. Initially, the drawings are for myself, to see how angles work and how light might be used, and what the director will require to block a scene with the actors. Once I have this technical framework for myself, I do a series of quite elaborate watercolours of the sets with detail such as props and furnishings. I usually do two angles for each set (a main view and a reverse). This is partly so the director can see what she or he's going to get, and also for everyone in the art department to see what we're aiming for. I know that some designers don't draw or paint, but I find it a definite advantage. I have built models – but in my experience, colleagues find it difficult to project themselves into a miniature cardboard space and no one really refers to them.

Being a production designer requires a wide range of skills and knowledge. Although that must now include an understanding of CGI, I believe one should still study the optical illusions that came out of painting and were exploited in theatre before being further developed by early film-makers such as Méliès. Although technology has changed, these tricks remain as effective – and cheap – as ever. CGI, by contrast, is still expensive. From personal experience, I believe that you get the most out of CGI by combining it with the old tricks. I'd also advise anyone who wants to be a production designer to become an observer. Don't just glance at the world, really look at it, and analyse it.

And remember, it's all lies, all the time!

biography

One of the most significant events to occur in world cinema in the 1980s was the breakthrough of the so-called Fifth Generation film-makers from China following the Cultural Revolution, during which the Chinese film industry was paralysed. Even if they were subject to censorship at home, the films of Zhang Yimou, in particular, were a revelation to audiences at film festivals worldwide and on the

cao jiuping

international art-house circuit. Jiuping has collaborated with Yimou on all his films as director, beginning with **Red Sorghum** (1987), and covering an extraordinary diversity of styles, from the stylisation of **Ju Dou** (1990) and **Raise the Red Lantern** (1991), to the fly-on-the-wall documentary look of **The Story of Qiu Ju** (1992); from the epic **To Live** (1994) which unfolds over four decades of turbulent Chinese history, to the atmospheric evocation of 1930s' Shanghai gangland in **Shanghai Triad** (1995). **Keep Cool** (1997), their most recent collaboration, represents yet another stylistic departure in its treatment of contemporary Beijing. Beyond his collaboration with Yimou, Jiuping also designed the first American-Chinese co-production, **Restless** (1998, Jule Gilfallan).

interview

I was nine years old when, on 14th September 1966, the Cultural Revolution turned my life upside down. Soldiers came to my childhood home, confiscated our possessions, burned my parents' photograph album and our family heirlooms. My school was closed. Left with no belongings and nothing to do during the day, I began to draw. I drew anything; I remember copying a cartoon from the newspaper of big-nosed American soldiers surrendering to Vietnamese troops. Later, when I was sent to work in the countryside like thousands of other teenagers, I got a reputation for drawing portraits of Mao Tse-tung, which made me the envy of others, and convinced me that I was a great artist...

When the Cultural Revolution ended in Autumn 1976, I was 19. I applied to the Xi'an art college; I was one of 20,000 applicants who also thought that they were artistic geniuses because they could draw portraits of Mao. My application, however, was successful, and I began to attend the college.

Meanwhile, I became aware of western literature and painting. Every week, I'd go to the library, and wash my hands in the finger-bowl supplied by the librarian before turning the pages of Japanese books about the great art collections of the world. I set my heart on becoming a painter, but my girlfriend at college was more interested in the cinema. She was subsequently accepted by the recently reopened Beijing Film Academy – whose new intake of students would become known as the "Fifth Generation" film-makers. Her interest in cinema made me take the medium more seriously. We volunteered to design film posters, in exchange for which we received complimentary tickets to see all the latest foreign films which were released in China. My eyes were opened to the world beyond China and also to the cinema as an art form. In 1983, I got a job as a scene painter at the Xi'an Film Studios, whose head Wu Tianming liberalised film production, attracting the Fifth Generation directors who had by now graduated from the Beijing Film Academy. I soon became an assistant art director and worked in this capacity on three films before becoming a production designer. In 1987, I began to work with Zhang Yimou on **Red Sorghum**.

The creative process with Zhang Yimou is based on our friendship and the close collaboration he inspires between director, writer, cinematographer, designer, costume designer and actors. We all discuss our respective work and help each other to resolve our problems – during this process, we often contribute changes or new ideas to the screenplay. I always research thoroughly the background of the film; I look for inspiration in literature, history, philosophy, painting and architecture. However, it is very important to balance research with intuitive response to the screenplay. One must be able to assimilate the information one gains from research but never allow it to dictate the design style. When Zhang Yimou proposed to set the story of **Ju Dou** in a dye factory, I was delighted because my father's family had once owned a dye house. I got my father to draw it from memory, and his rough drawing became the basis for the design of the dye house in the film. While talking to my father about the dye house, I became aware that we could make the different coloured dyes into an integral part of the story, interrelating the colours with the emotional dynamics. We produced a book of fabric swatches with different colours to help us work out the colour scheme for the textiles and costumes. At the beginning of the film we featured pale colours, and we made them progressively brighter and more vivid to reflect the story's passions. Then at the funeral which ends the film, the colours disappeared; as in a traditional Chinese funeral, Ju Dou and Tin Chang wore white clothes and carried a white flag. The only colour was the red coffin of Yinshan, the old proprietor of the dye house, whose tyranny had provoked the incestuous passion of the lovers and caused the fateful story to unfold.

I like to create a very strong sense of realism in my work, and for this reason, I prefer to build sets on location rather than in the studio. When I find a location that I feel is right for the film, it becomes a source of inspiration for the design. I get no such inspiration from standing on an empty studio stage. When we were preparing **Raise the Red Lantern**, we

(1–3) **Ju Dou**: The expressionistic design of the dye house was based on a rough sketch that Jiuping's father drew of the family's dye house. "It was in Sam Yen village in the heart of China, and it produced textiles decorated with folkloric colours and designs. In 1936, the Sim Hoy Railway built a station near the village, and suddenly western goods and colours were readily available. Many local businesses, including the dye house, suffered." Within the film's dye house, Jiuping sought to make the colours of the dyes reflect the turbulent passions of the film's story.

cao jiuping

(1–2) **Raise the Red Lantern**: The central design motif is the red paper lanterns used by the master to designate which of his wives he wished to sleep with each night. Jiuping thought of the lanterns as the all-seeing witness of the retributive tragedy that unfolds among the stone catwalks and courtyards of the estate. The passing seasons also play a vital part in the story, with critical scenes taking place in the snow. The film crew waited more than a month for real snow, after fake snow proved unsatisfactory.

3

5

4

6

7

8

9

(3–9) **To Live** was an epic vision of modern Chinese history and its impact on a family over 30 years. The sprawling action was unified by the traditional shadow puppet theatre (6–7) which reappears throughout the story. With its many locations and periods, the film represented a huge design challenge: "We were building on several major sets simultaneously in different provinces. We spent three months transforming a 1990s' business street into a 1940s' period location (8). We converted an old theatre into a casino. We prepared the battlefield for the civil war sequence (3), bringing in tanks and munitions. It was a very personal film for all of us, because the story reflected our own experience."

production design & art direction

(1–5) **Shanghai Triad**: 1930s' Shanghai interiors were shot in the studio and converted locations such as the youth recreation centre used for the nightclub scenes (1–2). The film's design contrasts the westernised, cosmopolitan atmosphere of the city and its underworld with the timeless rural landscape which serves as the setting for the climax (5). (6–7) **The Story of Qiu Ju**: Jiuping wanted to capture the simple beauty of rural life, evoked by such props as the spices and water chestnuts hanging from timber frames (6).

scouted for locations all over China, and although I did find some potential locations (including one which we ultimately rejected for **Raise the Red Lantern** but would use two years later as the gambler's house in **To Live**), I wasn't really happy with any of them. Just before we were about to return to Beijing, I suddenly remembered a photograph I had seen of the Chou Family Castle Village outside Taiyuan in the Shanxi province, and suggested we fly there on the way home. As soon as we arrived in this former manor house with its interconnecting courtyards, I knew we had found the right place – I had a sixth sense that Zhang Yimou (who hadn't come with us on the recce) was telling me, "This is the one". Once owned by a wealthy clan which was ousted by the Revolution, it had become a Communist Party school, which is why it was in such good condition; my main job as designer on the film was to restore all the correct period details. As with **Ju Dou**, colour played an important role; I created a contrast between the red of the lanterns (which I made) and the neutral colours elsewhere. I wanted it to feel as if these lanterns hanging in the darkness were the true witnesses of the unfolding tragedy.

The lanterns were the important detail to emphasise in the story of **Raise the Red Lantern**; in **Shanghai Triad**, we focused on the details of the doorways, because so much of the story is revealed through the mysterious events witnessed by the young peasant boy Shuisheng through open doors. Doors were an important motif in another respect: only by going through them can the characters find their way out of Shanghai's underworld maze.

Raise the Red Lantern was a very stylised film, like an opera. **The Story of Qiu Ju** was much more documentary in approach. About 50% of the film was shot using hidden cameras; because they could potentially see everything in Qiu Ju's village, we had to dress every detail of the village meticulously. We wanted to evoke the simplicity and beauty of the rural lifestyle depicted by the story. I always work closely with the costume designer; we exchange our research and show each other our preliminary sketches for the film. I often help to choose the materials and colours of the costumes. This is important because of all the design elements in a film, the clothes worn by the actors are most likely to be seen in close up or featured in the foreground of a shot. I also make a special effort to understand how the cinematographer visualises the film. Once I know what he wants to do, I like to surprise him by providing him with props and materials that will help his compositions – not all of which he will necessarily use (perhaps I should learn to be more frugal).

I like to create a strong atmosphere through a film's design, and that is why I spend a lot of time working with the prop-maker to create authentic props in order to communicate the right mood. I also like to use posters and paintings on the walls to evoke the atmosphere of the setting (the posters of Mao in **To Live**, for example, or the show posters in **Shanghai Triad**). In real life, such things are around us all the time, but we take them for granted. On screen, you can use these details to give the audience a heightened awareness of the film's setting and period.

biography

In his teens, Thomas worked at the Society Hill Playhouse in Philadelphia, performing a variety of tasks from hanging lights to painting scenery. He went on to study theatre design at Boston University. A protégé of two other designers featured in this volume, Richard Sylbert and Patrizia von Brandenstein, Thomas came to prominence as a production designer in his own right through his collaboration with Spike

wynn thomas

Lee which includes **She's Gotta Have It** (1986), **School Daze** (1988), **Do the Right Thing** (1989), **Mo' Better Blues** (1990), **Jungle Fever** (1991), **Malcolm X** (1992), **Crooklyn** (1994) and **He Got Game** (1999). It is a common danger for a designer to be typecast, or thought of only in connection with one director, but Thomas has avoided these pitfalls by diversifying in his recent filmography, while remaining based in New York: **A Bronx Tale** (1993, Robert De Niro), **To Wong Foo, Thanks for Everything, Julie Newmar** (1995, Beeban Kidron), **Mars Attacks!** (1996, Tim Burton), **Wag the Dog** (1997, Barry Levinson) and **Analyze This** (1999, Harold Ramis).

interview

My background is in theatre (I was a set designer), but I had always loved movies and since my theatre career was not developing the way I thought it should, I decided that I wanted to pursue film work. However, it was difficult breaking into the industry. My theatre experience did not count for much and no one was willing to give me a break. Finally, in frustration, I decided to offer my services for free to Richard Sylbert who was in New York designing **The Cotton Club**. What was supposed to be a two-week stint turned into a six-month job. Subsequently, Sylbert recommended me to Patrizia von Brandenstein, who was looking for an assistant for **Beat Street**, a movie about break-dancing. Observing at close hand how these two designers handled the politics of film-making was an amazing life lesson. Meanwhile, going from a huge studio picture straight on to a smaller, location-based film, was also an invaluable experience. This background gave me a strong foundation, but in time I grew bored with being chained to the drafting board and excluded from the

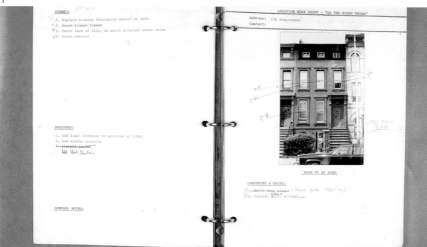

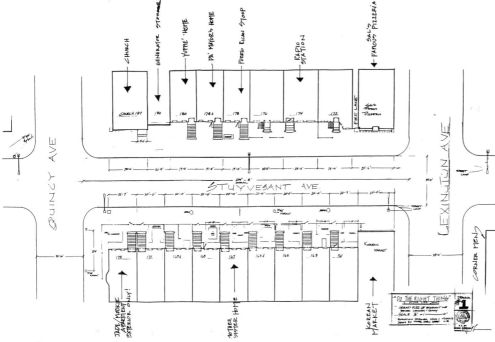

(1–4) **Do the Right Thing**: (3) Plan for the street set. (2) Thomas photographed each building on the block selected for the location, making notes on what needed to be done to it by the art department. (1) The fire-engine red wall was the backdrop for the old timers who acted as the film's Greek chorus. "My colour choices came out of my thinking, we're going to be on this block for two hours; what kind of twist can I give it to make it look interesting?"

creative decision-making. I began to look for opportunities to design low-budget films. One day, I met a graduate from NYU's film school who'd come to interview for a director's assistant post on **Beat Street**. We got talking; he was intrigued to meet me – at the time there weren't any African-Americans working as art directors. At the end of our conversation, he said, "maybe we can work together some day." His name was Spike Lee. My first film with Spike was a project called **Messenger**. The producer withdrew his money the Friday before the Monday we were supposed to start shooting. The next summer, Spike began to plan a smaller movie which he intended to finance himself with his grandmother's savings. **She's Gotta Have It** had two weeks' prep for a 12-day shoot, which I had to juggle with my day job as an assistant on **Brighton Beach Memoirs**. The budget was $22,000 (the art department budget was $800); it was a labour of love, everyone worked for the joy of it. As luck would have it, the film went on to glory and I went along for the ride with Spike as he ascended.

My theatrical background has greatly influenced my work in film. Stage designers think more conceptually than their counterparts in film, who tend to think in terms of realism. In the theatre, there's also a greater respect for the written word. The script is sacrosanct, it is the source from which all life springs. As a result, I've always felt that the solution to every design problem can be found in the script. When I'm reading a script, I'm not just focusing on the words, but also on the feelings they provoke in me. These are my raw materials, and determine what shapes and textures I will eventually use, and

most critically, what colours (colour for me is strictly a response to the emotional world of the script). When I'm talking to students, I always ask them, "How do you want the movie to feel?", because it's the feelings evoked by the world you create on the screen that an audience is left with. This is why my design process always starts with a conscious effort to articulate my emotional response to the script on paper, and then suggest a conceptual framework to translate that response in design terms. Production design is about how you can tell "the story" in the most appropriate visual terms. It's important to "support" the story/script, as well as the director. An early defining moment in my collaboration with Spike Lee came when we were thinking about Nola Darling's bed in **She's Gotta Have It**. Spike's feeling was, well, a bed is a bed is a bed. Mine was that we could use the bed to say something about this woman for whom physical and sensual pleasures were very important. Ultimately I spent about half my budget creating a bed that resembled an altar, with the candles and the open-framed backboard. Spike cites this as the moment when he really began to understand that art direction was a tool which could help him to define the characters in his films.

The production designer articulates the visual framework for the entire film. All parts should be working within that framework. I will always try to be as clear as possible about my approach to the entire film. In an ideal world, the director, production designer and cinematographer should be able to exchange ideas freely in the effort to find a visual vocabulary for the film, with no fear of treading on each other's territory.

production design & art direction

11 July 1989

Hello Ernest,

I hope this letter finds you in good health and spirits. These are just a few notes and impressions from my first meeting with Spike.

My Feelings on BENEATH THE UNDERDOG

As the name implies, I think the club should be on the lower level of a building... The basement. However, I want to avoid the basement "low-ceiling feeling." I want you guys to have the option of high angle shots. So the club will have higher ceilings than normal... And columns for visual and physical support of the ceiling.

Spike feels that the club is old... and should have a seating capacity of 150 people. I personally think that jazz clubs are too dark and neither Spike nor I want the movie to feel/ look like "Bird". So I'm fooling around with the idea of designing the club in what I'm calling an Afro-Chinese motif. This will enable me to give the walls and columns some texture and relief. (i.e. capital on top of the columns that are sculpted faces or shapes. This motif would also give me the option of using bold colors. Some reds, oranges, turquoises, blues, etc.

There will be a few jazz themed murals. (Has there ever been a Lee/ Dickerson/Thomas movie without a mural?)... Probably in the entrance of the club, on the ceiling and maybe the bathroom.

The club should have the feeling of a small nightclub. The exterior local should have a sense of being located in the village. The alley- should be a classic backstage alley. Lots of brick, scoop lamps, ...dramatic moody!

BLEEK'S LOFT

Spike and I had different points of view on Bleek's loft. He doesn't want the loft to be too "High-Style". Bleek is not that successful. We compromised- the loft will have some style. I have to be careful not to go too far. My feeling is that Bleek had a girlfriend who was a "decorator-type"- who "did" his apt. I don't feel that he would live in an undone or raw space. This is a man who likes things in order and in place.

1

I do feel that the loft should be an open space. The camera should be able to flow (Like A Jazz Tune) from one area to another without interruption. Ideally I'd like to divide the space up by using textured glass brick walls. This is a good and dramatic surface to shoot actors against...(As in love-making scene- good silhoutte possibilities and Bleek playing his horn.) Also one can light behind the brick- which will give us those "surreal" moments that we know we are going to want.

I see the loft in mono-chromatic colors (grey-white/ black-white) with splashes of color. Some old furniture- (A wonderful wicker armchair) mixed in with a modern Italian leather sofa. A colorful tiffany lamp. It's an open room with the possibility of pools of colored light- splashes of color. I think the John Coltrane mural/poster should be an impressionistic painting. And the willie Mays poster should be part of a collection of baseball memorbilia- with lots of stuff from the negro league!

The locations of Bleek's loft was also an issue that Spike and I did not resolve. I feel the loft should be in the Brooklyn Heights area with a view of Manhattan. (i.e. The watertower area.) Actually, I think the location of the loft will depend on what we will be able to find in Brooklyn. And my instincts tell me that there aren't too many loft spaces in Brooklyn.

That's it for now. This is just the beginning of a visual concept for the film. Please share all your thoughts and impressions with me. Meanwhile I hope things are going well on your film. Be well.

Wynn

2

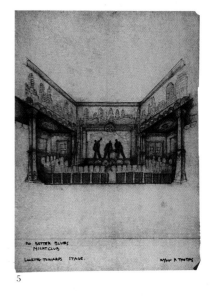

THE VERY 1ST THUMBNAIL SKETCHS FOR MO'BETTER CLUB

3

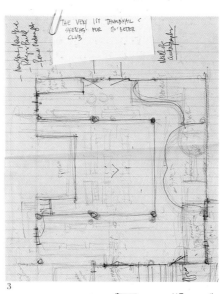

MO BETTER BLUES NIGHTCLUB

LOOKING TOWARDS STAGE.

Wynn A. Thomas

5

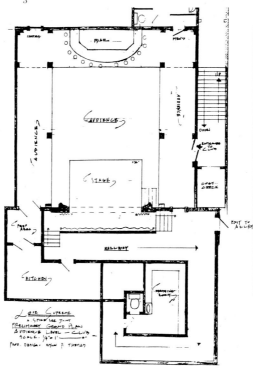

4

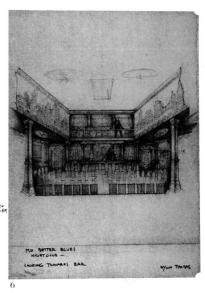

MO BETTER BLUES NIGHTCLUB —

LOOKING TOWARDS BAR

Wynn Thomas

6

9

10

11

7

8

(1–14) **Mo' Better Blues**: The design process of the Beneath the Underdog jazz club illustrates how Thomas works on a set: (1–2) his letter to D.P. Ernest Dickerson articulates his conceptual framework; (3) a rough plan followed by (4) a scale floor plan and (5–6) drawings (Thomas follows the example of Richard Sylbert, drawing up all such technical plans himself to give a true sense of scale and size); (7–8) stage and bar views of the finished club; (9–14) designing and building the set: snapshots of fabric swatches and the art department at work.

12

13

14

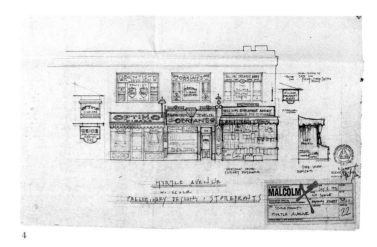

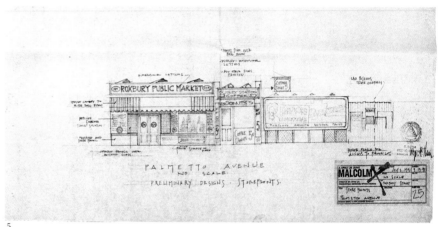

(1–9) **Malcolm X**: The opening scene, showing Malcolm's arrival in Harlem, cost around $1m. The New York location was restored to look as it would have done in the 1940s. (1–3) References for street fittings from Thomas' research folder. (4–5) Elevations for the buildings in the scene and (7–9) storyboard. "The opening act of the film was intended to be the most colourful portion of the film, almost like a 1940s' Technicolor film, vibrant with colour."

7

8

MALCOLM X

MALCOLM ARRIVES IN HARLEM - 125 ST. TRAIN STATION

Wynn P. Thomas

9

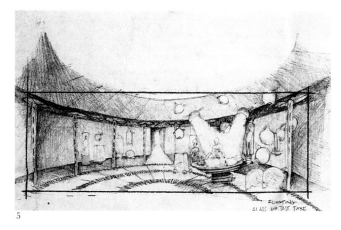

7

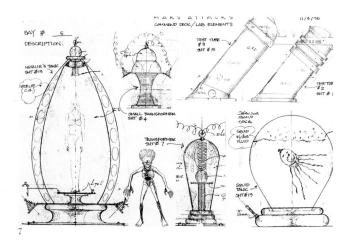

5

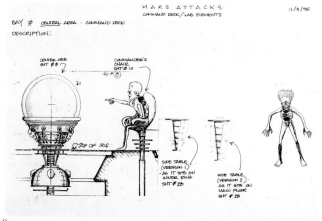

6

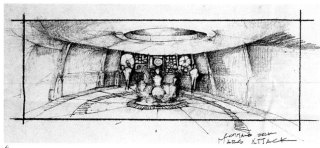

1

2

3

4

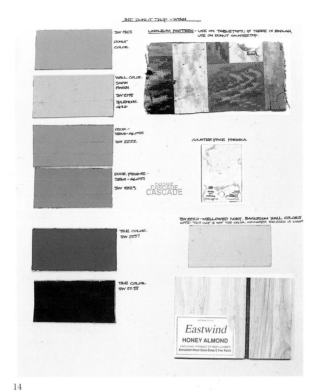

14

9

10

11

12

13

15

(1–15) **Mars Attacks!**: (1–2) "A lot of my design decisions were influenced by futuristic illustrations from the 1920s and '30s." (5) Early sketch for Martian spaceship command deck and (6) final design. (7–8) Drawings for command deck units including orb camera device from which Martian leader broadcasts to earth, as per (3–4) storyboard. Thomas used circular shapes as a motif which was repeated throughout the film: from flying saucers to sets such as the War-Room (11–13) to the Perkinsville location set (15) with its giant donut. (14) Colours, fabrics and textures selected by Thomas for the interior of the donut shop. (9–10) Location shots of a gas station and a distillery Thomas took when scouting in the mid-West for another film (**To Wong Foo, Thanks for Everything, Julie Newmar**) provided the inspiration for the Perkinsville set.

Such was the collaboration I enjoyed over eight films with Spike (who is great at allowing all the key players to make their contributions) and Ernest Dickerson (a great D.P. with a real love and knowledge of art direction). My relationship with the costume designer is different on each film; there is usually a great deal of talk about colour and texture. Of course the end goal is to support each other's work. Sometimes I will be the strong partner in this relationship – for example, my colour choices will dominate. On other occasions, I will deliberately restrain the set design to enable the costume to stand out. On **Mars Attacks!**, for example, I designed the "Kennedy Room" in the White House – scene of presidential seductions – so that it would allow the female Martian with her amazing dress and hairstyle to dominate.

I find that the design process is the same whether you're working on a low- or big-budget film. When you work on a low budget, the most important element is finding a location that will provide you with scale, line and texture, and a sense of drama. For **She's Gotta Have It**, we wanted a loft space for Nola's apartment, but the lofts we looked at lacked originality; they all shared the same floor plan which failed to inspire us. Finally, we came across the upper floor of a restaurant located at the base of Brooklyn Bridge. It was being used as a storage space, but it had these great, almost religious windows which fitted my concept of Nola's apartment as her "temple". Contrary to what some believe, location-scouting and location-designing is never easy. The location has to accommodate not only the aesthetic demands of the film, but also any number of practical considerations. For **Do the Right Thing**, the conceptual idea was to create a desert within the city, where the colours would be either very intense (as in the fire-engine red wall) or earthbound, and where there would be a complete absence of vegetation (no escape from the heat). As the whole film was set on one block, we also wanted the location to be visually stimulating in terms of architectural details. On the practical level, we needed a block with a lot of vacant lots where I could build the sets required for the film. Furthermore, the geographical relationships between these sets had to conform to the script so that the action would be able to unfold as intended (for example, the pizzeria had to be opposite the Korean market). We were extremely fortunate to find somewhere that met all these criteria.

I enjoy doing work that has an element of theatricality to it. Spike Lee's characters always are larger than life, with big passions, which I try to reflect visually. **Malcolm X** was an epic undertaking, but it struck me that Malcolm's journey unfolded in three acts, and by giving each act a different tonality, we were able to give the film a sense of visual unity. I gave each act a different tonality. The first was about Malcolm as a flamboyant young man, full of life, which we sought to represent with a 1940s' Technicolor feeling, making it the most vibrantly colourful section of the film. The second act represented a kind of rebirthing; during it, Malcolm is imprisoned and goes through a great deal of growth. We bled the colour from the design, giving the film a fairly monochromatic look. The absence of colour helped to emphasise the character's introspection. And in the third act,

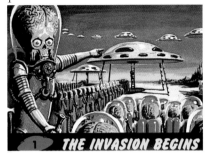

(1–7) Mars Attacks!: Director Tim Burton gave Thomas a complete set of the 1960s' trading cards on which the film was based (2–4). Their influence on the film's story and design can be seen in the production illustrations (5–7) for the climactic battle. "By the time we came to shoot the final destruction near the end of the schedule, we were running out of money. It would have cost too much to build these sets on the stage, so we had to try to find locations which were already partially destroyed or in a state of dilapidation."

1

2

3

4

5

6

7

8

9

10

11

(1–11) **To Wong Foo, Thanks for Everything, Julie Newmar**: "The design concept was The Wizard of Oz in reverse. The story starts in 'Oz' (Manhattan, where we depicted the drag queen milieu as larger than life and full of colour) and ends up in 'Kansas' – we found an isolated, almost monochromatic-looking small town in Nebraska". (10) Model for the drag queen show at Webster Hall and (1–9) references collected for Vida's apartment: "I try to define characters through the environment they live in. I put together a folder for every set which includes potential furniture, pieces of fabric, set decorating ideas, treatments for windows and floors. When I sit down to design the set, I draw my inspiration from the folder."

Malcolm comes into his own. Now he is a natural leader, at peace with himself; the look became similarly grounded, with the colour palette dominated by very natural, earthy colours (browns, beiges, greens).

Once I have determined the conceptual framework for a film with the director, I will put a folder together of visual material for every set in the film. It might include research such as illustrations from magazines or photographs taken on location scouts; it will also include potential furniture choices, swatches of fabric that I think have the right feeling, and anything that I feel relates the particular set to the overall concept. I also include set-decorating ideas – colours, window and floor treatments and so on. When I sit down to design the set, I draw my inspiration from the material in the folder. This approach helps me to build up an environment through which I can define the character who lives or works there, using the tools of my trade – line, shape, colour and texture. "Character design" is a very under-appreciated aspect of production design; again, it's a way of filling out the subtext and also telling the audience about aspects of the character that aren't specifically part of the dramatic action. I always ask the actors to come to the set several days before they start shooting. Denzel Washington actually lived for a couple of days in his loft on **Mo' Better Blues**. I encourage them to explore the space, open the drawers and look inside; I always provide the sort of stuff their characters might have to be dealing with, paperwork in a desk, for example. In **Do the Right Thing**, the actors had to get to know the pizzeria set so that they could make it appear as if they'd worked there for

years. They were all asked if there was anyone they wanted to see in the "Wall of Fame" (Danny Aiello, as it happened, was delighted because he knew most of the celebrities we'd preselected). I think it's important that there's a point where a set ceases to be a world I have designed and begins to become the world the actors live in. As a designer, your approach has to be flexible. It so happened that my sense of theatricality coincided with Spike Lee's, but it wouldn't have been appropriate for other directors or projects. Robert De Niro, for whom I designed **A Bronx Tale**, is fanatical about keeping things realistic. "Is this how they would do it for real?" was a constant question. **Wag the Dog** also demanded a level of realism in order to make the satire play effectively; I consciously avoided design which "commented" on the characters or situations. **Mars Attacks!** called for deliberate stylisation rather than character design. The movie is about the threat of destruction to the planet. I used repetition of circular forms and tried to create iconic images of the world that was under threat (the Mid-West heartland, for example, or the crassness of Las Vegas).

I never advise people about how to approach design because I think everybody has to find their own method, and you can only begin to articulate that with experience. However, to anyone who finds it difficult to break into the industry, I would always suggest you try to work as an unpaid volunteer for the very best production designer you can find. It's a way of getting a foot in the door. If that designer likes you, chances are they'll hire you on their next project. It's an investment in your own career.

biography

Like Jan Roelfs, with whom he worked in partnership for ten years, van Os worked as an interior designer before becoming involved in the Dutch film industry. The two designers combined the work of production designer and art director with van Os taking a more conceptual role, and Roelfs more involved with the technical execution. After the international success of **Orlando**, they worked together briefly in

ben van os

interview

Hollywood on the ill-fated **Dark Blood** (production was closed down after its star River Phoenix died). Soon thereafter, the partnership split when Roelfs decided to continue working in the U.S., while van Os returned to Europe. Van Os began his collaboration with Peter Greenaway on **A Zed & Two Noughts (ZOO)** (1985), followed by **Drowning by Numbers** (1988), **The Cook, the Thief, His Wife and Her Lover** (1989), **Prospero's Books** (1991) and **The Baby of Macon** (1993), as well as many of the director's short films. Apart from continuing to design films in his native Holland, van Os has also worked on a number of international co-productions including **Orlando** (1992, Sally Potter), **Vincent & Theo** (1990, Robert Altman), **The Gambler** (1997, Károly Makk) and **Alegría** (1998, Franco Dragone, based on Cirque du Soleil's production).

I would have no hesitation about advising any aspiring production designer to study art and architecture. It gave me an invaluable technical background, although when I was studying, I never dreamt I'd work in film myself. I was an interior designer for 12 years before one day being asked to furnish a villa for a film shoot. However, the owner of the villa suddenly took it into his head that film was evil and refused us permission to use the location. The result was that I was landed with the task of reproducing the interior of the villa in the studio. To my amazement and surprise, I was suddenly making a film. The producer Kees Kasander had worked with Peter Greenaway on **The Draughtsman's Contract**, and he asked me to meet the director.

As an interior designer, I approached my work in a fairly minimalistic way. When designing, I always used a grid which enabled me to divide the space into a series of visual lines. I found almost immediately that the same process was

1

2

3

4

5

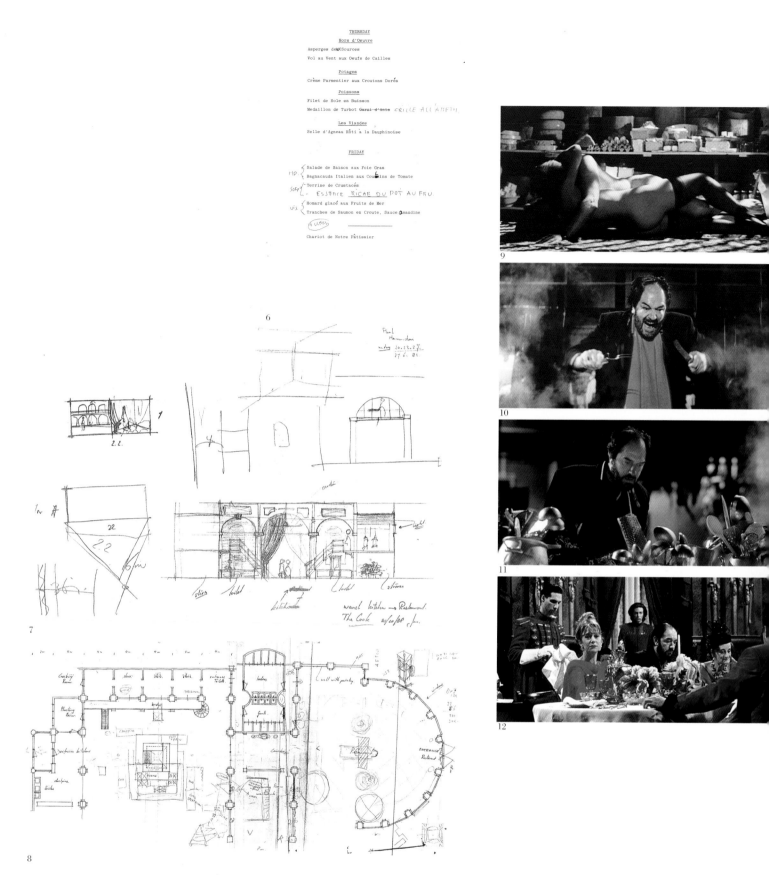

(1–12) **The Cook, the Thief, His Wife and Her Lover**: the design process for the composite restaurant set; (1–2) references for the exterior and the interior; (3–5) pages from van Os' workbooks show painting references, fabric swatches for soft furnishings, Polaroids of potential props and references for architectural elements. (7) Rough sketch for kitchen and restaurant and (8) ground plan showing the four main areas of the set: exterior, kitchen, restaurant and toilet. The space was designed to facilitate long tracking shots. (6) Copy for restaurant menu. (9–12) Colour was applied symbolically in the decor and lighting.

1

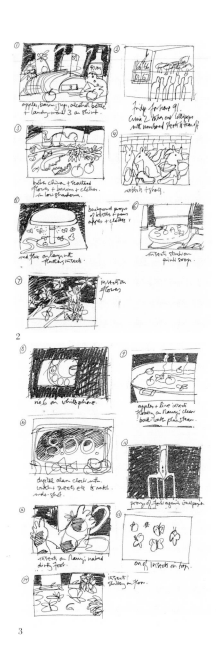

2

His collaboration with director Peter Greenaway and D.P. Sacha Vierney allowed van Os to develop a stylised design aesthetic characterised by symmetrical compositions and layered settings. "Many directors and D.P.s just think in terms of foreground and background. Sacha Vierney taught me to think of several layers to create depth and richness." (2–6) Sketched storyboard for **Drowning by Numbers**.

3

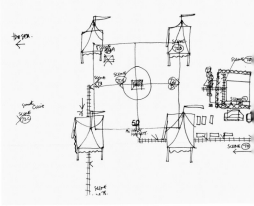

4

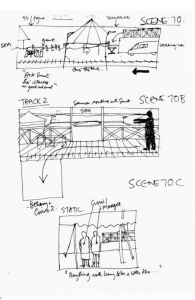

5

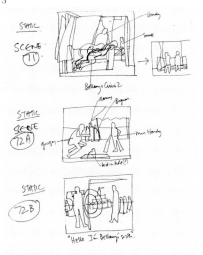

6

well-suited to Peter Greenaway's tableau-style compositions, especially in **ZOO** where the idea of line and symmetry was one of the script's themes. My aesthetic approach to film design was also influenced by the way Peter used colour; we experimented with colour schemes on **ZOO** and **Drowning by Numbers**, but he really pushed the idea more boldly when we began to work on **The Cook, the Thief, His Wife and Her Lover**. Red in the restaurant to evoke decadence; blue in the exterior set suggested the city; green in the kitchen represented what was new and organic and growing; white in the toilets symbolised purity and innocence; yellow characterised the Lover's antique books. Peter applies colour symbolically (he cannot work without symbols!), but it can also be used to structure a film visually. On **Orlando**, I used colour to characterise the different periods and locations dramatised in the film: I wanted to make the Elizabethan era as rich as possible, so I used a lot of reds and golds; whereas the transitional scenes on the ice were dominated by greys and silvers. In the Turkish sequences, I used yellow, and for Victorian England, green. I also applied colour in **The Arabian Nights** in order to code the different stories which Scheherezade recounts; because the film jumps between the stories, colour is a means of identifying each story for the audience.

I always paid a great deal of attention to where the light came from when I worked as an interior designer and light has become even more important to me in film. I regard the source of light as the basis for set design. Sacha Vierney, the D.P. on Peter Greenaway's films, has been a huge influence on my work. I've never known anyone else who handles light so beautifully, and yet he is a quiet, shy personality, always receptive to other people's ideas. His cinematography is very painterly; he lights in layers, giving the image great depth and richness. This has encouraged me as a designer similarly to layer my sets, so that there are different fields in the image from foreground to background, a style well-suited to large open-plan spaces such as we had on **The Cook, the Thief, His Wife and Her Lover**. Another key influence in how I have learned to think about light is the Italian designer Fortuny, who chose his fabrics on the basis of how they reflected light. I am fascinated by the way different materials catch light.

I am not interested in reproducing the real world. In **Alegría**, there was a scene set in the red-light district of Amsterdam. The director's initial impulse was to shoot it in the actual location, but I fought the idea because it seemed too obvious, and I didn't feel the picturesque canal background was appropriate to the tone of the story. I wanted to give it a more urban feel and suggested that we use a section of the Olympic stadium in Amsterdam, which is a very strong, sculptural concrete form. It gave an almost abstract impression of the city, into which we then built the prostitutes' boom-boom boxes. The same film also called for a Salvation Army clothing warehouse; the obvious idea was to find a real warehouse and fill it with racks of clothing. Again, I gravitated to a less literal image, choosing instead to build a huge ramp on to which I scattered thousands of kilos of old clothes, which the characters sorted through during the scene.

1

2

3

4

5

6

7

8

9

10

11

12

13

14

15

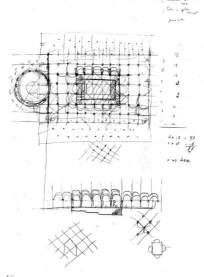

16

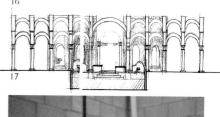

17

(1–18) **Prospero's Books**: "Peter Greenaway wanted to create the most advanced pop video ever made: a literary pop video for the big screen." (1–4) The film required 75 sets (including 38 on a large scale). (1) Prospero's staircase was modelled on that of the Lorenzo de Medici library in Florence (5). "We had ten artists working on 25 prop books over eight weeks." (7–9) Reference pictures collated by van Os for (10) one of the books. In order to achieve the film's set requirements on a budget of $500,000, van Os created one basic structure whose design was inspired by the Great Mosque in Córdoba (15). "We built a set of so many columns over 48 square metres in a hangar in Holland and we changed it every day, repainting it, redressing it according to the demands of each scene." (16) Plan for the set, (17) elevation and (18) model. (11–12) The swimming pool was used for Prospero's palace and (13) for Caliban's grotto.

18

I like to be able to work with abstraction, to stylise, and as a designer I'm very lucky to have been able to work with directors who are happy to go in that direction.

Cinematographer, production designer, costume designer – we all have to work together with the director to bring the script to life. With a director like Peter Greenaway, so much of the film's vision is already in the script – props, colours, symbols, camera movement. Despite his visual precision, however, Peter always says, "Surprise me". My design process always starts with the first reading of the script; I immediately begin to visualise it in my head as I read, and the design rarely changes very much from those first impressions. I often look at visual references. Peter always specifies his influences from painting (Franz Hals for **The Cook, the Thief, His Wife and Her Lover** for example; or Rembrandt for **The Baby of Macon**), but often, by happy coincidence, I find a film will correspond with a particular interest or influence of my own. For example, **ZOO** was set partly in Rotterdam Zoo, whose architect was Syboldt Van Ravenstein. Before working on the film, I had long been interested in his work, and introduced Peter to other examples of it in the city – a beautiful little theatre, an office interior and private houses. Peter was delighted – their baroque style was entirely appropriate to the film, and we used many of them as locations, dressing them with furniture designed by the same architect which was in a museum in Utrecht.

Similarly, one of my bibles is 'Architecture Without Architects', a book featuring architecture created by tribes and peoples in different landscapes all over the world. When I was asked to do **The Arabian Nights**, I suddenly found an appropriate context in which to use some of these places as locations – the long high desert houses made out of mud in Yemen. While researching the historical background for a project, I often find inspiration in books: for **The Gambler**, I didn't want a conventional 19th-century apartment because I knew the light source would be limited. From a book, I learned of an old palace that had been converted into apartments – which gave me the idea of creating the film's apartment in an old ballroom. This gave me the opportunity to feature much bigger windows and a section of the dome as the ceiling, both of which created more interesting possibilities for the lighting.

When I saw Scorsese's **The Age of Innocence**, I felt the production suffered from having too much money. I appreciated the research that had gone into it, and the precision with which the etiquette of the time was observed, but I felt that the recreation of the period setting in all its detail killed the film. I saw all the silverware on the tables and knew how many thousands of dollars it cost to rent. Personally, I am never impressed by the size of a budget, and I think that having a lower budget can force one to think more creatively. The script of **Prospero's Books** called for 75 sets (of which 38 were on a big scale) – impossible to achieve on our art department budget (around $500,000). So I decided to use one basic space which could be revamped, repainted and redressed according to the different set requirements. This approach – which I've used on other films – gives me much

1

2

4

(1–4) **The Baby of Macon**: "I did a lot of research into life in the Medici court, not because I wanted to reproduce history, but to give me a grip on the atmosphere." (1–3) The theatrical design and cinematography of the film was influenced by the golden age of Dutch painting in the 17th century, particularly Rembrandt.

ben van os

3

1

(3–4) Fabric swatches for the soft furnishings in **The Baby of Macon**. "I have to research and buy my own materials for a set. I need to see them and be able to touch them before I know whether they are right or not." Van Os is influenced by the Italian designer Fortuny (he collaborated on an exhibition about him with Peter Greenaway in Italy): "All his designs are based on light effects – how different fabrics receive and reflect light."

2

3

4

more creative control over how I spend my budget. I will allocate a lot of money to create the basic structure (but a lot less than I would if I was creating several separate sets), and then use the remainder for materials and props.

When I design, I tend to work very rapidly – I don't like giving myself the chance to have second thoughts. I start by making small-scale sketches for myself, and then I draw up more detailed technical plans. I don't make presentational drawings (unless required to do so by the financiers) because they don't give a reliable impression of the set. Many directors find it difficult to "read" technical plans, however, so I always make a model. Apart from giving the director a better idea of the space, a model is also very useful when I'm thinking about how to adapt a single space or structure to make several sets, as with **Prospero's Books**. It also allows the director and the D.P. to experiment with the lighting and shooting possibilities.

After **Orlando** was nominated for an Oscar for its art direction, I had the opportunity to work on Hollywood studio projects; but I do not like the industry system. There is a very rigid division of labour, which limits what the designer is and isn't allowed to do. I want to be able to be involved in every aspect of the design process; I want to be able to dress the set to my own satisfaction (in Hollywood, the designer is not allowed to climb up a ladder to change something himself). I want to have the freedom to be able to go out and buy my own materials and props. I cannot explain to a prop buyer what I need in advance. I need to go to a market, or an antiques shop

(where the most interesting things are often not on display, but in the basement), and look for something that surprises me. I need to see it and touch it to be sure that it is right for the film. In Europe, the production designer has more freedom to enter into every aspect of a film's design.

Drawing from my childhood is very important in what I do. I like to look at the world as if through the eyes of a child, to whom everything is new. When I was a boy of five, I used to make miniature settings for fairy-tales out of clay; today, at 54, I'm essentially doing the same thing and I hope I'll be doing it for the rest of my life. It amazes me that you can go somewhere like Uzbekistan (where we shot part of **Orlando**), and find film studios, art directors, costume designers – and realise that whatever the cultural differences between us, we all speak the same visual language. I love the collaborative aspect of our work – this simply doesn't exist if you are an interior designer. Often I am moved to tears when I watch shooting begin on a completed set and see how the cinematographer has illuminated it and what the actors are doing. Even after 15 years' working in film, I'm still fascinated by the process of building a project as a team and watching it grow.

biography

Beard emerged as an art director in the 1980s, when he began his long-term collaboration with Terry Gilliam. They first worked together on Monty Python's **Life of Brian**, for which Gilliam was production designer, and their collaboration continued on other Python films and Gilliam's short, **The Crimson Pearl Assurance**. Beard was art director on **Brazil** (1985), although he contributed much to the film's

john beard

design, and was still designing and building large sets for the film long after production designer Norman Garwood had moved on to another project. During the '80s, Beard also designed music videos for directors such as Steve Barron, Russell Mulcahy and Julien Temple with artists including David Bowie, the Rolling Stones and U2. Beard's feature films as production designer are: **Absolute Beginners** (1986, Julien Temple), **The Last Temptation of Christ** (1988, Martin Scorsese), **Map of the Human Heart** (1992, Vincent Ward), **The Browning Version** (1994, Mike Figgis), **Hackers** (1995) and **The Wings of the Dove** (1997) both for Iain Softley, and **The Lost Son** (1999, Chris Menges). In 1999, he resumed his collaboration with Terry Gilliam for **The Man Who Killed Don Quixote**. A self-professed "low-key designer", Beard believes the production designer is in essence the leader of a team.

interview

As an interior design student at Kingston College in London, I studied set design as part of the course. Subsequently, I won a Royal Society of Art's bursary in Television Set Design and was offered a job by Thames Television. I went for a day's work experience, but was disappointed. After the competitive and fashionable atmosphere of college, I found the prospect of working as a junior assistant making models of someone else's designs very restrictive to my ambition and enthusiasm. So I spent the next two years freelancing as an exhibition and shop designer. Then, one slack summer season while driving coast-to-coast in the States, I met Brian Eatwell, an English production designer who lived in L.A. He offered me a job as his assistant designing Marty Feldman's **The Last Remake of Beau Geste** in Europe. My one-to-one relationship with him was very different to my experience at Thames, and this time, I was hooked. It was a very lucky break, because in the late-'70s, the film industry was very unionised and difficult to enter. If you did manage to penetrate it, you had to spend

1

2

3

4

5

6

(1–12) **Brazil**: "Terry Gilliam wanted the film to look retro-futuristic, and I had a lot of comics and magazines from the 1930s (1–3) which we used as reference material for the vehicles in the film (4). The ideas they illustrated were bold, pure and clean." (5–6) Exterior of Sam's work place and the model which was constructed and rigged for the scene where the block is blown up. Beard designed the film's extraordinary dream sequence (10–12), working from Gilliam's original storyboard (7–9).

years training as a draughtsman before being given design responsibilities, whereas Brian had given me opportunities from the start. One of my first jobs was designing assorted false legs for Peter Ustinov, including a diamante dancing one and another which was a working cannon...

I was fortunate to collaborate with two directors whose different approaches gave me a very strong foundation for designing in film. It may seem surprising, given his reputation since **The Adventures of Baron Munchausen**, but Terry Gilliam has always been capable of achieving fantastic visual results for much less money than anyone else because he always knows where the set needs to be huge and where it needs to be detailed. He disliked time, effort and expense being wasted where it would not be seen. All his early films look as if they cost two or three times as much as they actually did. He encouraged me to believe that it is always possible to work on a large scale. The other director who influenced me was Nic Roeg, who I worked for on **Bad Timing** and **Eureka**. Nic focused on everything that contributed to an understanding of the characters. More than anyone else I have worked for, he believed that you should know what art a character would have on their walls, what books they would read and even what music they would listen to. It was a more intimate and realistic approach than Terry's, but equally valuable to me when I began to work as production designer on very different films. Several factors are likely to influence my choice of projects as a designer. It might be a fantastic design project like **Brazil** or **Absolute Beginners** (studio-based films usually offer the best design

opportunities). It might be a director with whom I like to collaborate with on a regular basis (like Iain Softley or Terry Gilliam); or a director I've always wanted to work with (Martin Scorsese on **The Last Temptation of Christ**). It might be an amazing location; or a terrific script. With any one project, it's usually a combination of two or three of these factors. I try to do a wide diversity of films – I don't like being pigeon-holed – and I've tended to gravitate towards post-war and futuristic material, because I find that this gives me more freedom for interpretation. I used to steer clear of period films, because I felt the accuracy required might be limiting in design terms. However, on **The Wings of the Dove**, Iain Softley encouraged me to create a richer but more realistic world than is usually seen in period films and to favour conceptual interpretation over a literal reproduction of London and Venice in 1910. Of course, one isn't always fortunate enough to be able to choose. As a designer, there are times when you're on a lucky streak (I had some fantastic opportunities back-to-back in the 1980s) and other times when the luck doesn't run with you. There are so many talented designers and relatively few really good projects; not a lot of us get to do great work on a regular basis throughout our careers.

On average, I'll have about three months of preparation on a film. That means roughly a month for conceptualisation and research, a month for drawing and planning and a month for building. I always enjoy the research period; it's an opportunity to learn about something I may not know much about – a period (for example, London in 1910 during the

1

2

3

4

5

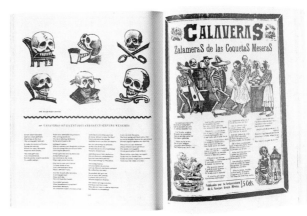

6

(1–8) **Absolute Beginners**: Influences as diverse as the Mexican "Day of the Dead" iconography (6) and Matisse cut-outs were evident in the Soho street and nightclub sets (7–8). "It was a distilled version of Soho. I took the bits which were visually most interesting and cut out everything else, creating a new street plan." Many of the views down side-streets were created with perspectivised models.

7

8

1

2

3

4

(1–6) **Absolute Beginners**: "Initially we intended to shoot the Notting Hill scenes in the actual location, but when the authorities discovered we were going to show race riots, permission was refused – so we found ourselves building it in the studio." (2) Construction on the back-lot at Shepperton Studios, and (4–6) scenes from the finished film. Roger Mayne's photographs of 1950s' London (3) were a key influence on the mood of these sequences.

5

6

upheaval caused by the building of the Underground was the setting for **The Wings of the Dove**), or a culture (the nomadic existence of the Inuits of Canada for **Map of the Human Heart**). If it's a film to be shot on location, the first recces offer a great opportunity to get to know the director and talk about the film: travelling in the Arctic Circle with Vincent Ward for **Map of the Human Heart**, or through the Atlas Mountains with Martin Scorsese for **The Last Temptation of Christ**. During the research period, I might also sit down with the director and look at other films – Scorsese screened Pasolini's **The Gospel According to Saint Matthew** as a reference for **The Last Temptation of Christ**; Julien Temple and I spent hours watching Vincente Minnelli musicals before **Absolute Beginners**. On **Brazil**, the research process was about creating a melting-pot of ideas and influences that could be integrated into Terry Gilliam's retro-futuristic concept. When he briefed me, Terry said, "I want the sum total of everybody's efforts; it won't look real if it's just one person designing it – a real world is designed by hundreds of people." I brought in friends from Kingston who were now graphic designers to create the background posters.

I'm amazed by other designers whose first drawings are incredibly precise and detailed, even featuring the props. I'd describe my own process as more sculptural by nature; I tend to think quite loosely at first about shape and scale and then allow the design to emerge gradually. I begin by plotting out the movement of the characters in the space. I imagine myself looking down on the scene unfolding in the script, and think about how characters will enter and exit, where they will sit,

what the distances between them might be at any given time in the scene. So my first design thought might be that we need a specific shape and size – before I actually think about what it will look like. In the 1930s and '40s, when the production designer had a lot of power, the art department would design a set in terms of specific camera angles. If the director or D.P. placed the camera a foot too far to the left or right, there'd be no set. Such limitations would never be accepted today. As a designer you really have to think about the camera potentially being able to see 360 degrees around the set.

I like to use models when I'm designing because they give a much clearer impression of the dimensions of a set than a drawing ever can. If you've only done a drawing, the director could well turn up on the set and say, "oh, I thought it would be bigger than this", whereas if you've done a model, it's very clear, and it enables the director to prepare the scene with far greater precision. This means money isn't wasted building things the camera won't focus on. When I designed the Soho street set for **Absolute Beginners**, I took the advice Terry Gilliam had once given me: use your budget where it counts; don't waste it detailing bits of doorways or windows that the audience will never see. If you're building sets on location, there's always a danger that a design you conceived back home won't translate when you're *in situ*. You can't find the right building materials, for example; or the location you were hoping to shoot in falls through. For this reason, I've learned to adapt my design ideas to the natural resources and construction methods wherever I happen to be working. On **The Last Temptation of Christ**, for example, we were

(1–17) **The Last Temptation of Christ**: Mary Magdalene's house was built in the ruins of a villa (4); here photographed after set construction and dressing (5) and in a scene from the film (1). The Garden of Gethsemane was to have been shot in a spectacular mountain location (6) before anxiety about bad weather forced Beard to redesign it at short notice in the cellar of an adobe fortress (7, 2). An olive grove and truck-loads of rocks were brought in for the exterior view. "I thrive on last-minute crises, it's part of making films. The adrenaline kicks in and you have to improvise a solution to the problem on the spot." Rather than strive to be "Biblical", the film's look was created by using indigenous materials and building methods of the Moroccan location. Natural dyes were used for costumes and furnishings (8–9).

Golgotha: establishing positions for the Crucifixion on location (10) before construction and shooting. The shot of Christ carrying the Cross (16) was based on Bosch's painting, 'The Ghent Christ Carrying the Cross'. During the Crucifixion, Christ experiences his last temptation — a dream of what might have been had he settled for love and domesticity with Mary. Beard and Scorsese decided the dream should have an idyllic quality — a lush, verdant, mountainous setting in contrast to the film's desert locations. Beard found such a location and built the set (13), only to be horrified when he returned days before shooting to find it was covered with snow (12). "The snow melted in time but it was very, very cold."

(1–4) **Map of the Human Heart**: "We had to get all the different period details right – the type of plane used by Arctic explorers in 1928, for example (4), or accurately portray the Inuit way of life (3). But we didn't want the film to feel too real. We took every opportunity to be more abstract or magical in our approach." (5–7) **The Wings of the Dove** updated Henry James' novel to 1910. Beard selected the location for the party scene (7) for its cerulean tiles: "Some locations or sets don't get much screen-time, so I like them to be simple, bold and memorable to help tell the story and so audiences won't blink and miss them." The Venice scenes (5–6) were designed and lit to give them an exotic atmosphere to contrast with the look of the gritty London street scenes.

shooting in Morocco, and we used the traditional methods of building with earth and sticks rather than sawn wood and plaster. Working like this can also support the film's aesthetic – in this case, it meant the buildings seemed to grow naturally out of the landscape and it gave us a palette of earthy colours that was appropriate to the nature of the story and the way Scorsese wanted to tell it; we tried to avoid a conventional "Biblical" approach. On **Map of the Human Heart**, we researched and used Inuit building methods and materials to recreate a traditional Inuit settlement of the past (they now live in Portakabin villages). The greatest compliment I had was that one woman aged 104 felt so at home that she didn't want to leave after we'd finished shooting.

I find it bizarre that some designers regard set design and dressing as separate aspects of our craft. Personally, I make no distinction between a background and what goes in front of it. I'm a very hands-on designer, and I feel it's important to be involved in every aspect of a film's design, including the set-dressing. But this does not mean that I have to dictate every detail of how the film should look. I was encouraged to make a creative contribution when I worked as an assistant and as an art director, and I like to offer the same opportunity to my team. Terry Gilliam taught me that a film is the sum total of everyone's efforts, and I know from experience that this sum total is what can make the difference between a good film and an exceptional film. I usually work with a very small art department, even on a big film, and I like to employ aspiring designers – with whom I can discuss what we're trying to accomplish – rather than an army of draughtsmen. I always give a brief, but encourage people to add to it and make it stronger, especially if they have a particular skill (as a painter or sculptor, for example).

However well prepared a film is, there are always last-minute problems. I enjoy the excitement and adrenaline of coping with such crises and improvising a solution. I also relish the challenge of going the extra mile to find the right location, rather than one that's already been featured in a dozen films, or to make a scene more extraordinary. I admire the way Vincent Ward goes to any lengths to get a shot he wants with no thought for his safety. On **The Wings of the Dove**, the producers and location people were telling Iain Softley and me that it would be impossible (a notion I don't accept) to get a wide shot of the Grand Canal at dawn after the Carnival. We went out at five in the morning and managed to get the few seconds of film we needed before 1990s' Venice intruded.

It's a great time to get into film-making. Since the 1970s and '80s, the unions' grip on the industry has loosened; the advent of pop promos and the increase in low-budget independent film production has created a lot more openings for designers coming out of film school. Nevertheless, I'd advise any aspiring production designer to get some experience as an assistant on two or three films with different directors. Whatever you may have learned in film school, this is how you really learn how design is applied and sets are used and get to see what works and what doesn't, what is and what isn't important, and also what kinds of unexpected problems occur. You can only learn such things by seeing them at first hand.

biography

Through his collaboration with Luc Besson, Weil has been an important figure in helping to restore the role of production design to prominence in French cinema. Director and designer first met in a confrontation over budget on a film that Besson was producing (**Kamikaze**, 1986, Didier Grousset); but good relations were restored by the time they first worked together on **Le Grand Bleu** (aka **The Big Blue**, 1988), and

dan weil

their collaboration continued with **Nikita** (1990), **Leon** (aka **The Professional**, 1994) and **The Fifth Element** (1997). Weil has also worked on more naturalistic and intimate location films such as **Hors la Vie** (1991, Maroun Bagdadi) and **Moi Ivan, Toi Abraham** (1993, Yolande Zauberman). A filmography remarkable for its diversity of genres and film-making styles, it also shows a designer who is capable of working in a variety of periods and locations. More recently, he designed **Total Eclipse** (1995, Agnieszka Holland), **Le Cousin** (1997, Alain Courneau) and **Belle Maman** (1999, Gabriel Aghion).

interview

As a result of the *nouvelle vague*, the role of the production designer and art department was rendered all but redundant in France. New wave film-makers shunned the studios and shot their films entirely on location. Directors and their assistants scouted for locations; and anyone could design the decor – a friend of the director, his cousin or girlfriend. After all, everyone has some degree of knowledge of how to decorate an apartment, and, from the late '50s until very recently, this is what film design in France was mostly about. This is why – for the first several years of my career – most of my studio-based experience was on commercials; my feature film work was nearly all on location.

I never intended to work in film; my background was in landscape design and architecture. I fell into my career by accident; through some friends, I became involved with an underground theatre company whose sets I designed for the next four years. During this period, I supported myself by

1

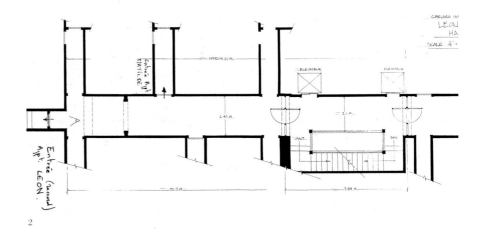

2

3

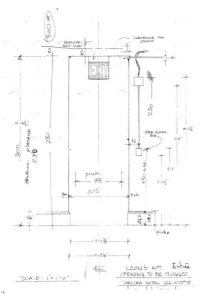

4

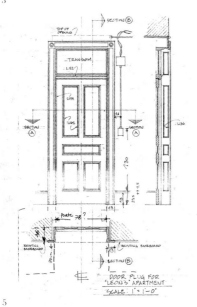

5

6

(1–10) **Leon**: "In some movies, the work of the production designer should not be noticed." This film is an object lesson in unobtrusive design which nevertheless created a powerful atmosphere and a sense of realism that gave credibility to the unlikely story of contract killer Leon (Jean Reno) and his 12-year-old partner Mathilda (Natalie Portman). The hallway of the apartment building where they live and where we first encounter Gary Oldman's villain was shot on location in New York. (1) Wallpaper sample; (2) floor plan of hall; (3) elevation of section to be converted into Leon's front door; (4) location photo of end of corridor, which Weil converted into the entrance to Leon's apartment; (5) elevation of section with door and (6) completed set in scene from film.

7

8

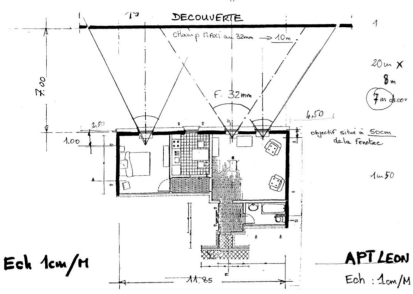

DECOUVERTE

Champ MAXI au 32mm → 10m

F. 32mm

7.00

20m X
3 m
7 m decou

4,50

objectif situé à 50cm
de la fenetre

1m50

2,80

1.00

Ech 1cm/M

11.85

APT LEON
Ech : 1cm/M

9

The interior of Leon's apartment was created as a studio set in Paris. (7) Recce photograph taken in New York as reference for the view from Leon's window. (8) Perspective model of view and (9) plan of apartment showing "view" in relation to the windows.

10

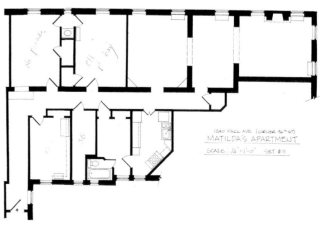

(1–9) **Leon**: Interior of Mathilda's apartment.
(1) Scallop shape for blinds chosen by Weil
from catalogue; (2–4) shots of finished
apartment; (5) paint colour chosen by Weil for
panelling, before ageing; (6) panelling
with paint colour, after ageing; (7) location
before art department went to work; (8)
the completed set; (9) floor plan.

APT MATHILDA (salon
cuisine LEON
(candle-wick)
Before AGEING

MATILDA'S APARTMENT
SCALE ¼"=1'-0"   SET #11

View from the Fatman's apartment in **Leon**'s opening sequence. (10–13) The Manhattan skyline was painted on a cyclorama (in the finished film, we see this view for under five seconds of screen-time).

working in advertising. Designing commercials was my film school. Firstly, I learned about precision. In commercials, one is obliged to be precise: you usually have only two shooting days, so you have to be decisive and well-prepared in terms of budget and schedule. You have to work to a precise brief which is non-negotiable: if the agency says it needs this shade of pink to sell Camembert, that's what you give them. Designing a commercial is not creative – it's purely technical; but that's what makes it a good school. I learned how to work with people and give them exactly what they wanted. Another benefit was the opportunity to collaborate with many different directors and crews (including great D.P.s like Tonino Delli Colli and Ennio Guarnieri). Furthermore, commercials allow the designer to experiment with different technologies and employ specialist craftsmen in the art department.

The big difference between working on a feature film and a commercial is that in advertising, the product is the bible, while in cinema, the script is the bible. Although the cult of the author-director exists in France (another legacy of the *nouvelle vague*), there is much more sense of common ownership on a film. On a commercial, the designer is a technician; on a film, a creative partner, along with the director and D.P. This means you can fight for something you believe in – not because it's what you want, but because you believe it's in the best interest of the film. As designers, however, we must remember that we are not artists so much as applied artists. Our work is always conditioned by external factors; the design of the film must address itself to questions posed by the script or by the director or D.P. For this reason, I

try not to let my own taste interfere with the design process. Say, for example, I have to design the interior of a concierge's lodge in a Parisian apartment building. The reality of such a place, decorated perhaps with kitschy ethnic trinkets, may not be aesthetically appealing – to my taste, at least – but my job is not to make something beautiful; it's to furnish the film with what is appropriate. Take the hitman in **Leon**, a character whose only interest is weaponry. Women, family, books, food, shopping: of no interest to him whatsoever. So how do you design his Manhattan apartment? Well, in all likelihood, he's rented it furnished and, given his character, he hasn't added anything to it. So as a designer, I'm thinking about how the owner of the apartment would have furnished it: probably with cheap, functional stuff that he wouldn't care about if it got damaged. Again, the design for such a set has nothing to do with my taste. **Leon** won several awards, but its design went largely unnoticed: people assumed it was all shot on location in New York. The reality is that we spent nine weeks in the studio in Paris. For me, the fact that the design didn't draw attention to itself was a compliment as great as any award.

I don't have hard and fast rules which I can always apply to my work. Each film, each script, requires its own set of ingredients. I call the sum total of everyone's efforts on a film "la mayonnaise". What is magical to me in movies is when you see the finished film and it works – and when that happens it's difficult to explain why or who exactly is responsible. It's never just the director, for example, or the designer. Each film has its own mayonnaise, and each time the recipe is different. The great production designer

(1–7) **Nikita**: "Director Luc Besson wanted a modern look, but if you try too hard to be modern, there's the danger that what is trendy today might rapidly date." To guard against such dating, Weil also integrates "timeless" decor within more modern design, such as the classic design of a French pharmacy (4–7). The cafeteria set (2): "I wanted to do something very '70s, using a lot of stainless steel."

Alexandre Trauner once said that our work was 60% research, 30% management and 10% creation. When I begin to work on a film, my first task is to research and build up an iconography for it. This involves gathering in visual elements such as references from painting or photography, my own sketches, swatches of fabric, colours, location snapshots, textural references to show details such as ageing. Sometimes a single book gives me the iconography for the entire film; for example, 'A Vanished World' – Roman Vishniac's collection of photographs of Polish-Jewish communities before they were destroyed by the Holocaust – was the foundation for the look of **Moi Ivan, Toi Abraham** (a film which depicts Catholic peasants, Jewish artisans and gypsies co-existing in rural Poland in the 1930s). When building up the iconography for a period film, there are potential pitfalls to avoid. Firstly, just because it's a period film, doesn't mean everything has to be old or aged down. People used to purchase new things for themselves, then as now (neither should everything look new and shiny; a balance is required). Secondly, a specific period setting does not oblige you to make everything typical of the era. It would be as nonsensical to make all the furnishings of a film set in 1870s' France typical of the Second Empire style as it would be to paint every apartment in a 1970s' film in psychedelic colours. While you obviously can't feature furnishings or props from a later era than that in which the film is set, the period will obviously still contain architectural and decorative elements from other times gone by. I don't find researching a period film difficult. It's always possible to find out what the bank-notes and coins of the past looked like; what kinds of writing implements people used, and so forth.

On a science fiction film, however, the entire world has to be reinvented.

For **The Fifth Element**, we set up a research studio for a year to develop a vision of New York in the future and its iconography. We employed twelve artists and illustrators, including Moebius and Jean-Claude Mézières, authors of the science fiction comics to which Luc Besson was addicted in his youth. Each week, we'd focus on a different theme: cars, apartments, money, food, domestic accessories, space travel. As the production designer, my role in this process was as much editorial as creative. Without dictating a design style, I wanted to make the design colloquial and ensure that we didn't entirely lose touch with reality; if you feature a flying car, the audience want to understand how it works. If you don't put a big engine under it, for example, they won't accept the idea. I also wanted to avoid sci-fi design clichés. Contemporary design is about simplifying the lines and operational features of the technology we live with; and yet most futuristic design one sees in the cinema complicates everything – there are flashing lights, dozens of buttons and switches, smoke. Getting the level of technology right was essential to me. We had a big discussion about telephones; can mobile phones get any smaller than they are now? No, because the distance between the receiver and mouthpiece cannot be diminished any further... Will everyone have videophones? No, because you might not necessarily always want to be seen by the person you're talking to... We sought to avoid making every aspect of the design hyper-modern; we kept the basic body of the New York cab, for example.

1

2

3

4

(1–2) **The Fifth Element**: Weil and his team of collaborators invented the iconography of a futuristic Manhattan. The designer ensured that their ideas were built on a base of recognisable reality: Cabs and police cars might fly, but they still conform to the classic design. The city's grid was retained: "Cities will evolve in the future, but they will build on what is already there." (3–4) **Le Grand Bleu**: Greek villages are normally built inland, but Luc Besson wanted to feature the sea view. Weil created a village on top of a cliff.

(1–7) **Total Eclipse**: Weil recreated the 1870 Paris setting by referring to the photographer Marville's extensive 1852 photographic study of the city. "I also looked at the Impressionists' early paintings." (1–2) Sketches for bar; (3) view through bar window before (4) and after; (5) bar location before (6) and after; (7) bar scene from the film.

Similarly, when thinking about Manhattan in the future, we felt that the basic grid structure of the city would not change. The real urban development would be to build underground (which is what has already begun to happen in Paris).

As with period and sci-fi films, so with contemporary films: you have to be careful about making everything too contemporary, too modern. This was the challenge of a film like **Nikita**. It's easy to be influenced by what is fashionable right now, but if you create something too up-to-date, quite possibly it will be dated by the time the film is released. And again, if you observe the world around you, you quickly see that not everything is new. The seats you see in most French cafés, for example, were designed in the 1870s. I was very influenced by American B movies from the 1950s while I designed **Nikita**. They never seem dated; they have a timeless quality – this is because they are not over-designed. Visual directors like Luc Besson (or Terry Gilliam or Ridley Scott) are potentially difficult collaborators because they know exactly what they want; however, their commitment to the image means they will always seek to capitalise on what you give them. Directors who aren't so interested by the visual possibilities of the medium may give you more freedom as a designer, but they won't necessarily exploit your work in such exciting ways. In our collaboration, Luc has always been very demanding, but also always receptive to my ideas. His approach to design is through camera composition and editing. He operates the camera himself, and when we begin to discuss a set, he will tell me how he intends to shoot the scene – how the actors will be framed, how the camera will reveal the action. He also talks about the visual relationship between two scenes: for example, he may request that at the end of one scene the character be in darkness before we cut to him in a bright, white environment. I love working this way, because it means that the design is serving the film-making, rather than supporting the director's – or my – personal taste. Creating a set is an organic process. In France, where art departments generally tend to be small, we treat our crews as collaborators. They are crafts-people and I expect them to be part of the creative process, so I will never hesitate to listen if a painter or carpenter wants to express an opinion about some detail of the design. In the last few years, I have worked internationally, which has made me aware of the cultural differences between crews in other countries. In the U.K., the process is more industrialised than in France, the crews tend to be more professional and efficient than in France, but the designer has less personal contact with them. There are also critical differences in working practices; if you're talking about paint colours, for example, you will refer to colour samples, whereas in France, choosing a colour is an editorial process. The painter will show me a yellow; if I find it too lemon I'll ask him to put some red in to make it warmer.

What advice would I give an aspiring production designer? When I was a student, the most important lesson I learned was to observe the world around me. I would say this applies to designers whatever their cultural background. Look and see. Everything around you is research that you may one day need to draw on.

biography

Anton Furst, widely regarded as one of the geniuses of contemporary film design, plucked Phelps from art college to work as an art director on **The Company of Wolves** (1984, Neil Jordan); subsequently, they collaborated on **Full Metal Jacket** (1987, Stanley Kubrick), **High Spirits** (1988, Neil Jordan) and **Batman** (1989, Tim Burton). Following the success of **Batman**, Furst was given a production deal at

nigel phelps

Columbia. He took Phelps with him to work as his in-house art director on the films he was developing, which included Michael Jackson's **MidKnight**. On 24th November 1991, Furst committed suicide – an incalculable loss to the film industry, and also personally for his protégé Phelps, who had moved with his family to L.A. Phelps soon emerged as a production designer in his own right. Graduating from commercials to feature films, he designed **Judge Dredd** (1995, Danny Cannon), **Alien Resurrection** (1997, Jean-Pierre Jeunet), **In Dreams** (1999, resuming his collaboration with Neil Jordan) and **The Bone Collector** (1999, Philip Noyce).

interview

My first ambition was to be a painter, but while I was an art student, my grant was stopped and so I had to find a job to pay my way through college. I met Paul Mayersburg, the screenwriter, who was then planning to direct his first film and needed to have the script storyboarded. I could draw, but didn't even know what a storyboard was. Paul made me watch two Orson Welles films, **Touch of Evil** and **The Lady from Shanghai**. "Watch the camera angles," he told me. "Look at the way it's lit and the shots are edited. Then read the script and illustrate it..." It was the best education in film I could have wished for. Paul introduced me to Anton Furst (who was going to design his film). Anton looked at my portfolio and offered me a job as an illustrator on **The Company of Wolves**. I had to choose between continuing my studies or working for Anton... I never painted again.

Anton was my mentor. He helped me develop an understanding of architecture. He taught me how to discern

(1–8) **The Company of Wolves**: Phelps' conceptual drawings. (1) Interior of Rosalind's house; (2) establishing view of Rosalind's village; (3) village well; (4) Grandmother's cottage; (5) village.

9

12

10

11

13

(9–15) **Full Metal Jacket**: Vietnam recreated in London's docklands for director Kubrick: (9, 12) Pagoda courtyard; (10, 13) Hue Street; (14) Ngoc Theatre; (15) Marine Corps Base Da Nang.

14

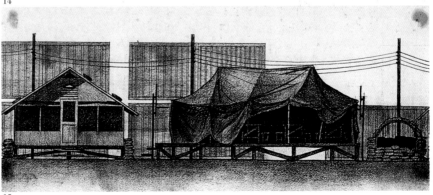

15

5

(1–7) **Batman**: (4) Initial design for City Hall; (3) Gotham City Square set (upper levels created in matte painting); (1) Batcave; (2, 5–7) interior and exterior of Flugelheim Art Museum.

1

6

2

7

3

4

between good and bad design. We worked together for ten years, doing commercials and features. My role initially was purely to sketch and draw. The way we worked together was established on **The Company of Wolves**; Anton showed me some painting references (Dürer, Bruegel, Bosch), then I made conceptual drawings to which he'd add brilliant little details and accents. And then I'd see the drawings being transformed – first into technical plans and then into actual sets. It was an amazing experience, looking at the finished set and thinking, I drew that. Soon after **The Company of Wolves**, we began working on **Full Metal Jacket**. For several months, we were a four-man art department working with Stanley Kubrick. You couldn't do a vague sketch for Stanley; it was absolutely critical that you knew the exact size of everything that you drew. Sketches would be turned into models, and then Stanley would photograph the models from every angle on different lenses so that every design permutation was thoroughly explored before construction started. Frequently, an idea would get nixed after you'd been working on it for several weeks – you couldn't be precious about anything you did. But exhaustive and exhausting though the process was, it gave me a technical understanding of film which has stood me in good stead ever since.

When I read a script, I let the words evoke their own images in my mind. Inevitably, there are subliminal influences and references at work when you visualise something. And when you read a script like **Alien Resurrection**, it's hard not to be thinking about the three visually brilliant films that preceded it. Although I find it useful to have references in mind, I never seek to reproduce them literally. I feel they are best used as triggers. On **Batman**, our vision of Gotham City was influenced by the tone of the 'Dark Knight' comics, and also by Andreas Feininger's photographs of New York buildings and the work of Japanese architect Shin Takamatsu. (**Blade Runner** was consciously avoided as a reference; no one was allowed to watch it while we were designing the film and neon was shunned altogether!) When I begin to design, I think in terms of an overall concept for the film rather than individual sets. Part of my job as a designer is to expand on the visual elements implicit in the script. This happens when I'm talking to the director and then when I start sketching.

For me, drawing is the key part of the design process. It's how I get the thing working. I've always drawn in black and white (I used to work in charcoal; now I use soft automatic pencils). This is partly a legacy of the days when there weren't colour photocopiers, but more important, I find black and white the best medium for describing line and shape, which help me define the structure of the design. Once the outline is in place, I start shading it – which is the equivalent of lighting a set. This is an integral part of the process, it's how you find out for yourself what's important to emphasise in the design. By back-lighting a building, for example, you're throwing the emphasis on the profile edge of the set – so forget about all the other details. Sketching for me is a process of discovery through trial and error – I habitually erase more than I keep. Thanks to laser-copy technology, I can now make my sketches thumbnail-size and then blow them up, which means that I can actually do more drawings.

(1–14) **Alien Resurrection**: From concept to screen: plans, drawings, storyboards and stills of (1–4) the flooded kitchen composite set for which a tank had to be built; (5–8) the clone storage facility; (9, 11–12) the alien egg chamber; (10) sketch of set where alien queen gives birth – which illustrates how Phelps recycled previous set elements as the chamber was constructed by chopping the basketball court set (13) in half and up-ending it. (14) Entrance into the Auriga spaceship. Phelps worked closely with D.P. Darius Khondji to integrate source lighting organically into the set structure: "We had lighting grilles above, below, from the side, and slots everywhere through which we could whoosh light into the set."

3

7

8

11

12

13

14

There are times when a set is just too three-dimensional and multi-layered to draw. If this is the case, it's better to go sculptural and make a model. Because my own models are pretty crude, I usually just draw plans and elevations and pass them on to a model-maker. A big film requires a lot of delegation. Invariably, there are people who are better-qualified than you are to take on certain aspects of the design. Julian Caldow, who drew the Batmobile on **Batman**, did all the vehicles and weapons for **Judge Dredd**. Chris Halls designed the Mean Machine and robot. Both are brilliant artists, but they are also great team players, which is essential because their work has to relate to the overall design concept.

There are many ways to make the design of a film cohesive, from the basic elements such as shape, texture and colour to the little details and accents you can put on the fittings of a set. I also like to use the same building blocks in the construction of different sets, a practice I picked up on **The Company of Wolves**, where Anton created the illusion of a huge forest mainly through scenic painting. There were very few trees, and it was relatively simple to move them about (they were made out of polystyrene) according to the composition required at any given time. I've applied this principle to everything I do; I like to be able to take the elements of a set and turn them back to front, upside down and inside out. I'll give them different textures or paint them different colours. On **Alien Resurrection**, I recycled two basic corridor structures in a variety of configurations to represent what in the script read as dozens of different sets. For example, I designed the basketball set so that it could be

split in half and up-ended to become the set in which the alien queen gives birth. Apart from being a very cost-effective way of working, this approach also helps to give the film's overall design an organic, cohesive quality. I also think carefully about how the design will be paced throughout a film. When I read the script of **Alien Resurrection**, for example, I was aware of the danger of making the film too claustrophobic. The story took place entirely on board spacecraft; there were none of the big vistas of other planets which so brilliantly counterpointed the enclosed spaces in the three previous **Alien** films. So I tried to introduce some huge areas in the Auriga ship which would serve a similar function and also allow the audience some breathing space.

As the set begins to be built and the different trades come in to do their work (riggers, carpenters, plasterers, painters, set dressers), the design process becomes editorial. I'm forever adapting and adjusting everything. When you initially choose the colour samples and finishes on a wall, for example, it's difficult to imagine what it's really going to look like on a whole wall. I might decide I want it to be aged down more than I'd initially planned. The same thing applies to the set dressing. I also take into account how the D.P. is going to shoot the film. Darius Khondji, with whom I worked on **Alien Resurrection** and **In Dreams**, uses a film process called ENR which really brings out the texture of the physical surfaces of the sets. It loves anything which has a rough, grainy weave to it; so after I've seen the camera tests, I might decide to capitalise on that and put more detail into the texture than I otherwise would.

© 1993 CINERGI PRODUCTIONS N.V.
ALL RIGHTS RESERVED

(1–7) **Judge Dredd**: (1) Megacity One building study: "The exclusive top level of the city was clean, metallic, reflective; then as you worked your way down the buildings to the blue collar street level, the look got progressively more aged and corroded." (2–3) Downtown Megacity. (5) Phelps' conceptual sketch: entrance to Halls of Justice. (6) Production illustration, Halls of Justice, by Matt Codd. (7) Gun design by Kevin Walker.

production design & art direction

2

6

7

10

11

14

(1–14) **In Dreams**: The script called for Phelps to visualise the protagonist Vivian's haunting underwater dreams. "It was hard to imagine these scenes because there's no reference material for anything like it; I designed them by thinking about how streets look in fog. The clarity of the water is going to play a big part in determining how much you can see. I knew there'd be a lot of fall-off, so I built houses close together and put as many trees in as possible so there'd always be stuff coming towards you as the camera moved through the water." (1) Illustration for underwater town and (2) town constructed in the same tank (in Mexico) used for **Titanic**. (3–4) Elevation and construction of town church. (5–6) Town building before and after ageing effects. (7) Town street during flooding. (8–11) Exterior of Vivian's house: sketch, model, ¹/₂ full scale house in tank before and after flooding. (12–14) Interior of Vivian's bedroom set before and after dressing, and flooded.

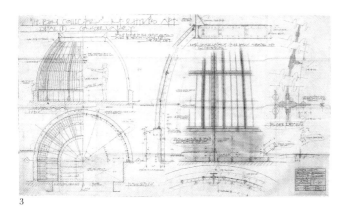

1

2

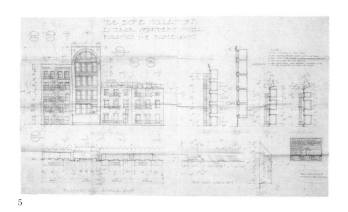

3

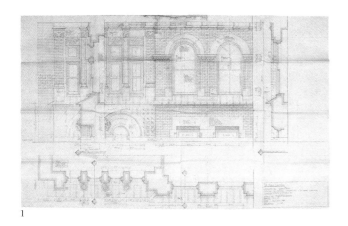

4

5

6

(1–6) **The Bone Collector**: Much of the film takes place in Denzel Washington's apartment where his forensic detective character is confined after being paralysed in a shooting. "We designed and built the whole apartment as a single composite set with two sets of windows that look on to Manhattan. Rather than using translite backings for the city views, we built perspectivised models for added realism – you can show light moving across them, you can have steam coming out of chimneys. Because we were shooting in the apartment for five weeks, we created visual variety by simulating diverse weather conditions outside. It's quite a challenge, sustaining the illusion of the perspective without the audience realising, it's a model!"

One of the lovely things about our work is that you never do the same thing twice. Each film is different, not just in terms of subject and content, but also because you'll be working with a different crew and specialists – like Pitof, the brilliant visual effects supervisor on **Alien Resurrection** – who have their own individual creative and technical strengths. This creates a unique chemistry on each film you work on. Something else I learned from Anton Furst is to be selective about what work you do. Following his example, I work on commercials so that I don't have to accept the first feature project that is offered to me. This allows me to be available when the right film comes along. Commercials have also enabled me to work with the new generation of film-makers (directors like Mark Romanek, Simon West and Michael Bay) who have all graduated from the medium into features. With each new film project, I like to seek out new design challenges. **In Dreams** was mostly a location film, but the way the story interwove its New England settings with the dark fantasy of the dreams was a terrific hook for me as a designer. Ultimately, though, my personal preference is for films which require ground-up, imaginative design – creating entire worlds in the studio.

glossary

PERSONNEL

Production designer: Head of art department, primarily responsible for giving a film a cohesive visual concept through the design of interior and exterior sets.

Art director: Works closely with the designer, supervising the execution of the designs for individual sets.

Scenic artist: Paints the images featured on scenic backdrops such as cycloramas.

Set decorator: Responsible for dressing a set with furniture, soft furnishings and props.

Prop master: Responsible for preparing all props required for a scene as required by the screenplay.

Prop buyer: Purchases or hires props and furniture, working under the supervision of the set decorator or production designer.

Props dresser: Positions props in a set prior to shooting.

Props stand-by: Repositions props in a set between each shot and each take.

Construction crew: The group of craftsmen (including plasterers, carpenters, painters, riggers and other specialist craftsmen) who build a set, working to the specifications detailed in technical plans or models supplied by the production designer and art director. The crew is headed by a construction co-ordinator.

Costume designer: Responsible for the design of clothes worn by actors in the film.

Director of photography: Head of camera department, responsible for lighting each set during a film shoot, and for all of the photographic elements of the film.

Location manager: Responsible for the initial scouting of locations (*see* **Location**) for a film, and then for hiring and administrating those finally selected by the film's director and production designer.

TECHNICAL TERMS

Ageing: The process of rendering a surface so that it gives the illusion of being old.

Back-lot: Area of studio grounds where exterior sets can be built.

Blocking: The technical rehearsal in which the actors' positions in relation to the set and camera are plotted out.

CGI (computer-generated imagery): The digital enhancement or manipulation of a film image.

Close-up: A shot cropped close to the head (and shoulders) of an actor.

Composite set: A set featuring a number of separate spaces through which a sequence of action unfolds.

Construction: The process of building the set according to the production designer's specifications.

Drafting: The process of drawing up technical plans and elevations to show what will be required in the construction of a set. These may be executed by the production designer or art director, or by draughtsmen.

Dressing: The process of decorating a set with furniture, soft furnishings and props according to the specifications of the production designer and set decorator.

Elevation: Scale drawing of a set made in projection on a vertical plane.

Exterior: An outside location for a scene, as designated by the screenplay.

Forced perspective: A technique used to give the illusion of depth; background elements that are supposed to look very distant are rendered in even more diminished scale while foreground elements are full size.

Gimbal: A device originally designed for use at sea which enabled equipment such as the compass or chronometer to maintain a horizontal position even when the ship was being pitched on rough seas.

Hand props: Props handled by the actors.

Interior: An indoor location for a scene, as designated by the screenplay.

Location: Any outdoor or indoor setting found in the real world (i.e. outside the studio lot) and subsequently adapted by the production designer to provide the set for a scene.

Long shot: A shot which reveals a large portion of the background setting.

Matte painting: A background painting which is composited with foreground live action shot separately (against a blue screen).

Miniature: A scale model of a large set which is combined optically with live action footage of the actors (shot separately) to create the finished image.

Model: A scale model built under the supervision of the production designer as a working tool to give a sense of the size and proportions of a set.

Perspective: The illusion of three dimensions created in two – like the canvas of a painting or a cinema screen.

Plan: Scale drawing of a set as viewed overhead.

Props: Objects and accessories featured in the dressing of a set. These may be made specifically for the film, or hired or purchased.

Scene: A self-contained unit of action that takes place in one setting, as laid out in the screenplay. A sequence of such units constitutes the dramatic action of the whole film.

Scenic painting: A large-scale painting representing reality in the background of a city or landscape.

Set: Any setting, interior or exterior, studio or location, which serves as the background for a scene.

Set-up: The position of the camera in relation to the set and action during a single shot, designed to cover a portion of a scene.

Source light: Refers to light which is intended to come from a particular source in a set – e.g. through a window or from a light such as a table lamp.

Stage: Large covered and sound-proofed space within a studio on which sets are built prior to shooting.

Storyboard: Sequence of drawings representing different shots which show how the action of a scene will unfold.

Studio: A factory for the production of films, containing a number of stages and a back-lot on which sets can be built, and a tank where water scenes can be shot; as well as offering a number of back-up resources (production and art department offices, actors' dressing rooms, cutting rooms, equipment hire companies, visual effects companies, construction facilities and paint-shops).

Trompe l'oeil: Generic term for variety of optical effects pioneered by painters during the Renaissance and designed to deceive the eye into believing that it is witnessing three-dimensional reality.

Visual effects: Any visual manipulation of the "reality" presented to the camera. This might be achieved in-camera (speeding up or slowing down the image, for example, shooting it in reverse or in double exposure), or on-set, through front- or rear-projection, or through compositing separately shot elements in an optical printer or through computer-generated imagery (CGI).

Wild (Wall or Ceiling): A part of a constructed set which can be removed to facilitate shooting or lighting a set-up.

picture credits

Courtesy of The Kobal Collection: p 6 **The Adventures of Baron Munchausen**, Columbia Tri-Star; p 12 **Vertigo**, Paramount; p 16 **The Sting**, Universal (2, 3); p 19 **To Kill a Mockingbird**, Universal (5); p 22 **Unforgiven**, Warner Bros. (1); p 29 **You Only Live Twice**, EON/UA (9, 10); p 30 **Thunderball**, Danjac/EON (4); p 32 **Chitty Chitty Bang Bang**, Warfield/United Artists (1); p 34 **The Madness of King George**, Sam Goldwyn/Channel Four/Close Call, photography by Firooz Zahedi (6); p 35 **The Madness of King George**, Sam Goldwyn/Channel Four/Close Call, photography by Firooz Zahedi (12); p 36 **Addams Family Values**, Paramount (1); p 38 **Dick Tracy**, Touchstone, photography by Peter Sorel; p 41 **Chinatown**, Paramount (2–4); p 42 **The Graduate**, Embassy (3); p 44 **Dick Tracy**, Touchstone (13); p 45 **Dick Tracy**, Touchstone, photography by Peter Sorel (7, 11); p 45 **Dick Tracy**, Touchstone (15); p 48 **The Name of the Rose**, Neue Constantin/ZDF, photography by Bob Willoughby; p 50 **The Canterbury Tales**, UA/PEA Prod/Prod Artistes Associes (4); p 53 **The Name of the Rose**, Neue Constantin/ZDF (11); p 55 **And the Ship Sails On**, RAI TV/Vides/Gaumont (1, 8); p 56 **The Adventures of Baron Munchausen**, Columbia Tri-Star (3); p 57 **The Adventures of Baron Munchausen**, Columbia Tri-Star (10); p 58 **Kundun**, Touchstone/Capra/De Fina, photography by Mario Tursi (4); p 59 **Kundun**, Touchstone/Capra/De Fina, photography by Mario Tursi (8); p 60 **Interview with the Vampire**, Geffen Pictures (1); p 62 **The Godfather Part III**, Paramount; p 64 **Apocalypse Now**, Zoetrope/UA (3); p 65 **Apocalypse Now**, Zoetrope/UA (8); p 66 **One from the Heart**, Zoetrope/Columbia (3); p 66 **The Godfather**, Paramount (4); p 66 **The Godfather Part III**, Paramount, photography by E. Lari (6); p 69 **Tucker: The Man and His Dreams**, Lucasfilm Ltd./Paramount, photography by Ralph Nelson Jr (1); p 70 **Tucker: The Man and His Dreams**, Lucasfilm Ltd./Paramount, photography by Ralph Nelson Jr (7); p 72 **The English Patient**, Tiger Moth/Miramax; p 74 **The Elephant Man**, Paramount (2); p 74 **Dangerous Liaisons**, Warner Bros. (4, 5); p 79 **Mary Reilly**, Tri-Star (12); p 82 **The Avengers**, Warner Bros., photography by David Appleby (1, 4); p 86 **Ragtime**, Paramount, photography by Bob Penn (2); p 87 **Silkwood**, 20th Century Fox (10); p 93 **The People vs. Larry Flynt**, Columbia Tri-Star (6, 7); p 96 **Schindler's List**, Universal; p 100 **Schindler's List**, Universal (7); p 101 **Schindler's List**, Universal (10); p 103 **Korczak**, Perspektywa/Regina Ziegler Filmprod (3); p 104 **Danton**, Les Films du Losange/Groupe X/Gaumont (6); p 105 **Danton**, Les Films du Losange/Groupe X/Gaumont (7, 9, 11); p 106 **Europa, Europa**, Les Films du Losange/CCC Filmkunst (1); p 108 **Fanny & Alexander**, Svensk/Filminstitut/Gaumont/Tobis; p 110 **Fanny & Alexander**, Svensk/Filminstitut/Gaumont/Tobis (2); p 122 **Caravaggio**, BFI/Channel 4/Ward-Jackson (1, 2); p 123 **Caravaggio**, BFI/Channel 4/Ward-Jackson (14, 15); p 124 **Edward II**, Working Title/BBC/BR Screen (1, 3, 8); p 136 **Raise the Red Lantern**, ERA International (1, 2); p 137 **To Live/Huozhe**, ERA/Shanghai Film Studio (4); p 140 **Malcolm X**, Warner Bros.; p 142 **Do the Right Thing**, Universal (1); p 146 **Malcolm X**, Warner Bros. (6); p 149 **Mars Attacks!**, Warner Bros., photography by Bruce Talamon (13); p 151 **Mars Attacks!**, Warner Bros., photography by Bruce Talamon (1); p 152 **To Wong Foo, Thanks for Everything, Julie Newmar**, Universal/Amblin, photography by Lorey Sebastian (11); p 157 **The Cook, the Thief, His Wife and Her Lover**, Allarts/Erato (9–11); p 158 **Drowning by Numbers**, Allarts (1); p 161 **Prospero's Books**, Allarts/Camera 1/Cinea (13); p 166 **Brazil**, 20th Century Fox; p 169 **Brazil**, 20th Century Fox (10); p 171 **Absolute Beginners**, Virgin/Goldcrest/Palace, photography by Graham Attwood (5); p 176 **Map of the Human Heart**, Working Title/Films Ariane/C4/... (1, 2); p 176 **The Wings of the Dove**, Miramax/Renaissance Films (5); p 178 **Leon**, Gaumont/Films du Dauphin, photography by Patrick Camboulive; p 180 **Leon**, Gaumont/Films du Dauphin, photography by Patrick Camboulive (6); p 181 **Leon**, Gaumont/Films du Dauphin, photography by Patrick Camboulive (10); p 185 **Nikita**, Gaumont/Cecchi Gor/Tiger (3); p 187 **The Fifth Element**, Columbia/Tri-Star (1, 2); p 188 **Total Eclipse**, Fit/Portman/K2/SFP (7); p 190 **Alien Resurrection**, 20th Century Fox, photography by Suzanne Tenner; p 192 **The Company of Wolves**, Palace/NFFC/ITC (6–8); p 193 **Full Metal Jacket**, Warner Bros. (11); p 194 **Batman**, Warner Bros./DC Comics (7); p 197 **Alien Resurrection**, 20th Century Fox, photography by Suzanne Tenner (4, 8); p 199 **Judge Dredd**, Cinergi Pictures, photography by Richard Blanshard (4).

Courtesy of the Ronald Grant Archive: p 21 **Unforgiven**, Warner Bros., Inc. (7); p 28 **Goldfinger**, EON Productions (5); p 66 **One from the Heart**, Zoetrope/Columbia (2); p 66 **The Godfather Part II**, Paramount (5); p 84 **Amadeus**, Orion; p 88 **Amadeus**, Orion (3); p 132 **To Live/Huozhe**, ERA/Shanghai Film Studio; p 135 **Ju Dou**, Tokuma Enterprises (1); p 137 **To Live/Huozhe**, ERA/Shanghai Film Studio (3, 5); p 138 **Shanghai Triad**, Shanghai Film Studio (1–5); p 138 **The Story of Qiu Ju**, Sil-Metropole (6, 7); p 157 **The Cook, the Thief, His Wife and Her Lover**, Allarts/Erato (12); p 160 **Prospero's Books**, Allarts/Camera 1/Cinea (1); p 164 **The Baby of Macon**, Allarts U.G.C. (2).

Visual material contributed by Henry Bumstead: p 13 Portrait shot; p 14 **Vertigo** (1–4), with thanks and acknowledgement to Paramount; p 15 **Vertigo** (5–12), with thanks and acknowledgement to Paramount; p 16 **The Sting** (1) illustration by Tom Wright, with thanks and acknowledgement to Universal; p 18–19 **To Kill a Mockingbird** (1) illustration by Dale Hennessey, (2–4, 6–9), with thanks and acknowledgement to Universal; p 21 **Unforgiven** (1–6, 8–10), with thanks and acknowledgement to Warner Bros.; p 22 **Unforgiven** (2–5), with thanks and acknowledgement to Warner Bros.

Visual material contributed by Ken Adam: p 24 **Goldfinger**, with thanks and acknowledgement to EON Productions; p 25 portrait shot from **Pennies From Heaven**, with thanks and acknowledgement to MGM; p 27 **Dr Strangelove** (1–7), with thanks and acknowledgement to Hawk Films Prod/Columbia; p 28 **Goldfinger** (1–4, 6), with thanks and acknowledgement to EON Productions; p 28 **Dr No** (7), with thanks and acknowledgement to United Artists; p 29 **You Only Live Twice** (8), with thanks and acknowledgement to EON/UA; p 30 **The Spy Who Loved Me** (1), with thanks and acknowledgement to EON Productions; p 30 **Thunderball** (2, 3), with thanks and acknowledgement to Danjac/EON; p 30 **Moonraker** (5–7), with thanks and acknowledgement to United Artists; p 32 **Chitty Chitty Bang Bang** (2), with thanks and acknowledgement to Warfield/United Artists; p 32 **Pennies From Heaven** (3), with thanks and acknowledgement to MGM; p 33 **Pennies From Heaven** (4–15), with thanks and acknowledgement to MGM; p 34 **The Madness of King George** (1–5), with thanks and acknowledgement to Sam Goldwyn/Channel Four/Close Call; p 35 **The Madness of King George** (7–11), with thanks and acknowledgement to Sam Goldwyn/Channel Four/Close Call; p 36 **Addams Family Values** (2–7), with thanks and acknowledgement to Paramount.

Visual material contributed by Richard Sylbert: p 39 portrait shot; p 41 **Chinatown** (1) illustration by Joe Hurley, (5), with thanks and acknowledgement to Paramount; p 42 **Carnal Knowledge** (1, 2) illustrations by Bill Major, with thanks and acknowledgement to Avco-Embassy; p 44 **Dick Tracy** (1, 2, 4, 5, 8, 9, 12, 14), with thanks and acknowledgement to Touchstone; p 45 **Dick Tracy** (3, 6, 10) illustrations by Bill Major, (16), with thanks and acknowledgement to Touchstone; p 46 **Carlito's Way** (1), with thanks and acknowledgement to Universal; p 46 **Mobsters** (3) illustration by Leon Harris, (2), with thanks and acknowledgement to Universal.

Visual material contributed by Dante Ferretti: p 49 Portrait shot from **The Name of the Rose**, photography by Mario Tursi, with thanks and acknowledgement to Neue Constantin/ZDF; p 50 **The Decameron** (1–3), with thanks and acknowledgement to PEA/Artistes Associes; p 50 **Arabian Nights** (5, 6), with thanks and acknowledgement to PEA; p 52 **The Name of the Rose** (1–4), (5–7) photography by Mario Tursi, with thanks and acknowledgement to Neue Constantin/ZDF; p 53 **The Name of the Rose** (8–10, 12, 13) photography by Mario Tursi, with thanks and acknowledgement to Neue Constantin/ZDF; p 55 **And the Ship Sails On** (2–7), with thanks and acknowledgement to RAI TV/Vides/Gaumont; p 56 **The Adventures of Baron Munchausen** (1, 2, 4), with thanks and acknowledgement to Columbia Tri-Star; p 57 **The Adventures of Baron Munchausen** (5–9), with thanks and acknowledgement to Columbia Tri-Star; p 58 **Kundun** (1–3, 5), with thanks and acknowledgement to Touchstone/Capra/De Fina; p 59 **Kundun** (6, 7, 10), (9) photography by Mario Tursi, with thanks and acknowledgement to Touchstone/Capra/De Fina; p 60 **Interview with the Vampire** (2–7), with thanks and acknowledgement to Geffen Pictures.

Visual material contributed by Dean Tavoularis: p 63 Portrait shot from **I Love Trouble**, with thanks and acknowledgement to Touchstone; p 64 **Apocalypse Now** (1, 2), with thanks and acknowledgement to Zoetrope/UA; p 65 **Apocalypse Now** (4–7), with thanks and acknowledgement to Zoetrope/UA; p 66 **One From the Heart** (1), with thanks and acknowledgement to Zoetrope/Columbia; p 69 **Tucker: The Man and His Dreams** (2–4), with thanks and acknowledgement to Lucasfilm Ltd./Paramount; p 70 **Tucker: The Man and His Dreams** (1–6), with thanks and acknowledgement to Lucasfilm Ltd./Paramount.

Visual material contributed by Stuart Craig: p 73 Portrait shot; p 74 **The Elephant Man** (1, 3), with thanks and acknowledgement to Paramount; p 76 **The Secret Garden** (1–8), with thanks and acknowledgement to AM Zoetrope/Warner Bros.; p 77 **The Secret Garden** (9) fabric swatches contributed by Stephenie MacMillan, (10–12), with thanks and acknowledgement to AM Zoetrope/Warner Bros.; p 78 **Mary Reilly** (1–6), with thanks and acknowledgement to Tri-Star; p 79 **Mary Reilly** (7–11), with thanks and acknowledgement to Tri-Star; p 81 **The English Patient** (1), (2, 3) contributed by Stephenie MacMillan, with thanks and acknowledgement to Tiger Moth/Miramax; p 82 **The Avengers** (2) fabric swatches contributed by Stephenie MacMillan, (3, 5–8), with thanks and acknowledgement to Warner Bros.

Visual material contributed by Patrizia von Brandenstein: p 85 Portrait shot; p 86 **Ragtime** (1, 3–8), with thanks and acknowledgement to Paramount; p 87 **Silkwood** (9, 11), with thanks and acknowledgement to 20th Century Fox; p 88 **Amadeus** (1, 2, 4–7), with thanks and acknowledgement to Orion; p 90 **Just Cause** (1–3) photography by John Snow, with thanks and acknowledgement to Warner Bros.; p 90 **The Untouchables** (4–6), with thanks and acknowledgement to Paramount; p 91 **The Quick and the Dead** (7–16) photography by John Snow, with thanks and acknowledgement to Tri-Star; p 93 **The People vs. Larry Flynt** (1–5) photography by John Snow, with thanks and acknowledgement to Columbia Tri-Star; p 94 **Man on the Moon** (1, 3, 5, 7) photography by John Snow, (2, 4, 6), with thanks and acknowledgement to Universal.

Visual material contributed by Allan Starski: p 97 Portrait shot; p 98 **Man of Marble** (1, 2, 5–7) photography by Renata Paschel, (3, 4), with thanks and acknowledgement to Film Polski; p 100 **Schindler's List** (1–6), with thanks and acknowledgement to Universal; p 101 **Schindler's List** (8, 9, 11–15), with thanks and acknowledgement to Universal; p 103 **Korczak** (1, 5, 6), (2, 4) sketches by Andrzej Wajda, with thanks and acknowledgement to Perspektywa/Regina Ziegler Filmprod; p 104 **Danton** (1, 2, 4, 5), (3) sketch by Andrzej Wajda, with thanks and acknowledgement to Les Films du Losange/Groupe X/Gaumont; p 105 **Danton** (8, 10), with thanks and acknowledgement to Les Films du Losange/Groupe X/Gaumont; p 106 **Europa, Europa** (3, 4) storyboard and sketch by Agnieska Holland, (2), with thanks and acknowledgement to Les Films du Losange/CCC Filmkunst.

Visual material contributed by Anna Asp: p 109 Portrait shot; p 110 **Fanny & Alexander** (1, 3–6), with thanks and acknowledgement to Svensk/Filminstitut/Gaumont/Tobis; p 112 **The Best Intentions** (1–7), with thanks and acknowledgement to Channel Four/Norsk Rikskringkasting; p 113 **The Best Intentions** (8–14), with thanks and acknowledgement to Channel Four/Norsk Rikskringkasting; p 115 **The Sacrifice** (1–7), with thanks and acknowledgement to Svensk Filminstitutet; p 116 **The House of the Spirits** (1–8), with thanks and acknowledgement to Neue Constantin/Spring Creek; p 117 **The House of the Spirits** (9–13), with thanks and acknowledgement to Neue Constantin/Spring Creek; p 118 **Jerusalem** (1–3), with thanks and acknowledgement to Sveriges Television/Svensk Filmindustri; p 118 **Les Misérables** (4–6), with thanks and acknowledgement to Mandalay Entertainment.

Visual material contributed by Christopher Hobbs: p 120 **Edward II**, with thanks and acknowledgement to Working Title/BBC/BR Screen; p 121 portrait shot; p 122 **Caravaggio** (3–9), with thanks and acknowledgement to BFI/Channel 4/Ward-Jackson; p 123 **Caravaggio** (10–13), with thanks and acknowledgement to BFI/Channel 4/Ward-Jackson; p 124 **Edward II** (2, 4–7), with thanks and acknowledgement to Working Title/BBC/BR Screen; p 126 **The Neon Bible** (1–8), with thanks and acknowledgement to Scala; p 127 **The Neon Bible** (9–14), with thanks and acknowledgement to Scala; p 129 **Velvet Goldmine** (1–9), with thanks and acknowledgement to Zenith; p 130 **Velvet Goldmine** (1–6), with thanks and acknowledgement to Zenith.

Visual material contributed by Cao Jiuping: p 133 Portrait shot; p 135 **Ju Dou** (2, 3), with thanks and acknowledgement to Tokuma Enterprises; p 137 **To Live/Houzhe** (6–9), with thanks and acknowledgement to ERA/Shanghai Film Studio.

Visual material contributed by Wynn Thomas: p 141 Portrait shot; p 142 **Do the Right Thing** (2–4), with thanks and acknowledgement to Universal; p 144 **Mo' Better Blues** (1–6, 9–11), with thanks and acknowledgement to Universal; p 145 **Mo' Better Blues** (7, 8, 12–14), with thanks and acknowledgement to Universal; p 146 **Malcolm X** (1–5), with thanks and acknowledgement to Warner Bros.; p 147 **Malcolm X** (7–9), with thanks and acknowledgement to Warner Bros.; p 148 **Mars Attacks!** (1–8), with thanks and acknowledgement to Warner Bros.; p 149 **Mars Attacks!** (9–12, 14, 15), with thanks and acknowledgement to Warner Bros.; p 151 **Mars Attacks!** (2–7), with thanks and acknowledgement to Warner Bros.; p 152 **To Wong Foo, Thanks for Everything, Julie Newmar** (1–10), with thanks and acknowledgement to Universal/Amblin.

Visual material contributed by Ben van Os: p 154 **The Baby of Macon**, with thanks and acknowledgement to Allarts U.G.C.; p 155 portrait shot; p 156 **The Cook, the Thief, His Wife and Her Lover** (1–5), with thanks and acknowledgement to Allarts/Erato; p 157 **The Cook, the Thief, His Wife and Her Lover** (6–8), with thanks and acknowledgement to Allarts/Erato; p 158 **Drowning by Numbers** (2–6), with thanks and acknowledgement to Allarts; p 160 **Prospero's Books** (2–10), with thanks and acknowledgement to Allarts/Camera 1/Cinea; p 161 **Prospero's Books** (11, 12, 14–18), with thanks and acknowledgement to Allarts/Camera 1/Cinea; p 163 **The Baby of Macon** (1–4), with thanks and acknowledgement to Allarts U.G.C.; p 164 **The Baby of Macon** (1, 3, 4), with thanks and acknowledgement to Allarts U.G.C.

Visual material contributed by John Beard: p 167 Portrait shot from **The Wings of the Dove**, with thanks and acknowledgement to Miramax/Renaissance Films; p 168 **Brazil** (1–6), with thanks and acknowledgement to 20th Century Fox; p 169 **Brazil** (7–9, 11, 12), with thanks and acknowledgement to 20th Century Fox; p 171 **Absolute Beginners** (1–4, 6–8), with thanks and acknowledgement to Virgin/Goldcrest/Palace; p 172 **Absolute Beginners** (1–6), with thanks and acknowledgement to Virgin/Goldcrest/Palace; p 174 **The Last Temptation of Christ** (1–9), with thanks and acknowledgement to Universal; p 175 **The Last Temptation of Christ** (10–17), with thanks and acknowledgement to Universal; p 176 **Map of the Human Heart** (3, 4), with thanks and acknowledgement to Working Title/Films Ariane/C4/... p 176 **The Wings of the Dove** (6, 7), with thanks and acknowledgement to Miramax/Renaissance Films.

Visual material contributed by Dan Weil: p 179 Portrait shot; p 180 **Leon** (1–5), with thanks and acknowledgement to Gaumont/Films du Dauphin; p 181 **Leon** (7–9), with thanks and acknowledgement to Gaumont/Films du Dauphin; p 182 **Leon** (1–9), with thanks and acknowledgement to Gaumont/Films du Dauphin; p 183 **Leon** (10–13), with thanks and acknowledgement to Gaumont/Films du Dauphin; p 185 **Nikita** (1, 2, 4–7), with thanks and acknowledgement to Gaumont/Cecchi Gor/Tiger; p 187 **The Big Blue** (3, 4), with thanks and acknowledgement to 20th Century Fox/Société Nouvelle des Etablissements Gaumont; p 188 **Total Eclipse** (1–6), with thanks and acknowledgement to Fit/Portman/K2/SFP.

Visual material contributed by Nigel Phelps: p 2 **Batman**, with thanks and acknowledgement to Warner Bros./DC Comics; p 191 portrait shot; p 192 **The Company of Wolves** (1–5), with thanks and acknowledgement to Palace/NFFC/ITC; p 193 **Full Metal Jacket** (9, 10, 12–15), with thanks and acknowledgement to Warner Bros.; p 194 **Batman** (1–6), with thanks and acknowledgement to Warner Bros./DC Comics; p 196 **Alien Resurrection** (1, 2, 5, 6, 9, 10), with thanks and acknowledgement to 20th Century Fox; p 197 **Alien Resurrection** (3, 7, 11) storyboard by Silvan Dupré, (12–14), with thanks and acknowledgement to 20th Century Fox; p 199 **Judge Dredd** (1–3, 5), (6) illustration by Matt Codd, (7) illustration by Kevin Walker, with thanks and acknowledgement to Cinergi Pictures; p 200 **In Dreams** (1, 3–5, 8, 9, 12, 13), with thanks and acknowledgement to Dreamworks SKG; p 201 **In Dreams** (2, 6, 7, 10, 11, 14), with thanks and acknowledgement to Dreamworks SKG; p 202 **The Bone Collector** (1–6), with thanks and acknowledgement to Universal.

index

production design & art direction